Conversation Pieces

out of the

Studio

The voice-over workshop for professional actors

Jeffrey Dreisbach

Conversation Pieces out of the Studio, *The* Voice-over Workshop for Professional Actors
copyright © 2011 Jeffrey Dreisbach

All photographs and cover design by Jeffrey Dreisbach

1. Voice-over Acting 2) Performing arts   I. Title

US $14.95

ISBN: 978-145750-479-2

Library of Congress Catalog No: Applied for

Published by: Dog Ear Publishing

Table of Contents

W ith the ever growing, limitless expansion of cyber-space, learning has been redefined and restructured as we know it. Virtual classrooms, blogs of information and online libraries have taken their rightful place as our latest methods for obtaining information. Even the art of publishing books has given way to handheld electronic readers in many cases. So the question now becomes *why write a book at all?* After all, if it's just a matter of finding information, then internet resources can certainly fit the bill. In the performing arts, the prevailing opinion is that there is really no way to teach through books alone. Sure, we can learn about various acting techniques, read "how to" manuals of information and even download scripts for auditions and rehearsals. Yet, there is much more value in having the experience of acting and voice acting with *each other*. What I have discovered in 25 years of teaching (in addition to being a professional actor) is that human interaction is essential to the growth of a performer. We need to have tangible evidence of our skill set by having face to face feedback and critiques that can only happen when sharing the same space of a theatre, studio or classroom. And yet...

I have incorporated several years of acting, voice-over's and teaching (workshops, classes, intensives, universities, training school programs, acting studios and high schools) to create this comprehensive *Voice-over workshop for actors*. While nothing can replace the interpersonal experience of a private coach, I am confident the information and *workshop workouts* will serve as both a guide and mentor on your journey as a voice-over actor. I also believe that by using this manual as a partner or collaborator (rather than reading a website or blog) will become a tangible reminder of the adage "words without deeds is dead". Therefore, work the exercises and scripts whenever you feel the need. Re-read chapters to boost your confidence level. Discover some new ways to keep yourself motivated. Finally, I entreat you to embrace the journey so that you may discover or perhaps reignite the joy of performing.

Thank you to the hundreds of students, educators, actors and friends who have, in no small part, enriched this book with their love, support and insight. Thank you for making **Conversation Pieces out of the Studio** part of your new skill set.

Jeffrey Dreisbach 2011

Prologue

Conversation Pieces out of the Studio is first and foremost a training manual for the professional actor or performer wishing to gain knowledge and insight into the world of voice-overs. Contained herein are workout pages for you to use, exercises to perform and practical information to accelerate your understanding of what voice-over's are all about. By studying each of the chapters and working on all of the projects, you will, no doubt, learn useful performance skills and become qualified to chart your own course for success in this fun and fascinating field. The reason for my confidence is simple: I have experienced countless positive results with students who have taken my workshops. Whether it was a university course or professional training school, actors who applied themselves often come away with tangible assets that "book" voice-over jobs.

In order to get the greatest benefit from this workshop, there are some assumptions that I am making about you, the reader. First, you are someone who has some performance background or experience. It isn't necessary for you to hold a degree, have major league credits or a killer announcer voice. Many concepts are more clearly understood if you have a performer's sensibilities. Second, you are able to make the time to work each of the assignments. This is not an overwhelming commitment of your time, but rather, every task must be completed for greatest effect. Actually, you can design you own schedule for the course. It is totally up to you. Third, while there is no requirement for this, having a way to record and replay the workshop's performance scripts would be useful. Nothing fancy, a tape recorder or computer a microphone is all you need.

Finally, reading the book in chronological order will, in effect, duplicate the learning methods that I have used in the classroom. I think this is best because it follows a logical sequence that is more easily digested than a hit or miss technique. The first chapter includes a definition, terminology and methods that are used to write commercial voice-overs. Exploring useful criteria for the audition and performance interpretation tools comes next. After that, we will examine the production elements that are used to make you sound your best. We will also look at animation voicing, narration scripting and casting yourself for a voice demonstration recording (demo). Lastly, we will visit the various business components necessary for voice-overs: marketing, promotions and getting the job will be addressed. I hope you enjoy our time together. I have loved combining my teaching experience and professional background into a workbook that you will, hopefully, find useful, informative and rewarding!

Introduction

It feels more like the waiting room of a dentist's office than a voice-over audition. About a half dozen actors, each with their newly crumpled scripts, nervously mouth the six word commercial with multiple "takes" in their heads. Each one is hoping to get the booking. Even the professionals in the room seem to exude the seriousness of Hamlet, wondering what will happen next. Suddenly, an adjacent door swings open and an intensely thin woman with glasses and clipboard ushers out an actor who has the grim expression of exhaustion and relief. He quickly exits the fear-laden den of the waiting room. "Next" is uttered by the obviously bored clipboard holder as another potential Hamlet enters the darkened inner chamber of the recording studio. This process continues for several hours until all of the hopeful performers have displayed their wares to the anonymous suits behind the studio glass. This scenario occurs in advertising agencies, casting directors' offices, audio studios and agents' offices on a regular basis.

Welcome to the world of the voice-over actor.

The recording studio is waiting for you as "next" is heard.

Performance Anxiety

O K, so this audition scene on the previous page may seem a bit dramatic. Yet, it is something I have heard many actors express and have even experienced in my own career. Granted, the performer's imagination and sensitivities can sometimes exaggerate the stressful reality in which we find ourselves. Even so, auditions and bookings can be fraught with nerve-racking experiences. With so much intensity, why would anyone want to do a voice-over?

The answer to that question can vary depending on who you ask. Newcomers believe it is easy money. In other words, "All I have to do is read a script in a funny voice and I can make big bucks!". Others may want to do voice-over work simply for the fun of it. I suppose, in truth, each reason is valid. Yes, there is the potential that serious money can be made. After all, there is an implied assumption that the celebrity voices we hear must be rolling in it. Why not us? And yes, it is true that recording a voice-over can be a fun experience. There are, however, some realities that should be addressed before you can realistically answer the question for yourself. That is what this *master class* is all about.

Using my experience, as both a voice-over actor and broadcast/performing arts educator, I will provide tips, techniques and strategies to propel you into clear understanding of the VO (voice-over) world. My wish is that you will come away with more confidence, skill and motivation. Some of the pages are informational, while others are meant for you to use as practice or rehearsal material, to be done in the privacy of your own space. There are sample scripts and *workbook workouts* with practical tools, discussions and explanations. By completing each section, you will be following methods that I have incorporated into the many workshops and classes I teach. I realize that there is no substitute for working with a performance coach in a class environment, yet, I believe you will find this book exceedingly helpful, whether you are a newcomer or a seasoned professional.

So...welcome to class. I hope you will have a fun-filled, useful, exciting time. If you stick with it then the nightmare waiting room scene will not be part of your story. Let's get started!

Exercises

Jeff's notebook

Workshop tools

Before we can even begin our class, I must first provide you with a definition of what a *voice-over* (VO) actually is. Sometimes actors do not fully appreciate the range of opportunities that exist for them because they have a preconceived notion of VO's being just an announcer for commercials. While it can include being an announcer, there is so much more. Think of the following, *"Heard but not seen"*. It means that every time you hear a voice: character, announcer, telephone prompt, video game, book on tape, toy, narrator, commercial, movie, radio, animation, public address or promo, *and not necessarily be seen*, you are listening to a voice-over. (The exception is when you re-voice yourself in a movie or TV job).

As the evolution of technology continues to accelerate at breakneck speed, the need for performance voice talent will also continue to expand. What is even more fascinating to me is that there have been few technological advances wherein the human voice is replaced with digitalization alone. You may come across some companies like banks or airlines using automated phone messaging prompts, but even then, individual words are provided by professional voice actors. The computer will assemble these individual words to make a sentence, yet, there is a very noticeable "electronic" quality that is clearly not human. You see, nothing as of yet can replace the dynamic warmth, emotional strength and frankly, humanness, that we humans possess.

So, while our focus on this workshop will be geared toward commercials, promos, animation, book narration or, more to the point, *performance techniques* for the voice actor, keep in mind the vast opportunities that this performance art could provide. You may have just winced when you read the word *art* in the last sentence. You may think this is a bit lofty on my part. After all, we are not talking Rembrandt or Mozart here. But I do feel quite strongly that when a performer gives their time, talent, skill, interpretation and therefore, uniqueness, to the performance, they are giving of themselves. It is the gift of giving that creates an artist. Like your fingerprints, no two voices are alike. Each one has unique qualities that cannot ever be replicated. That is why I am always thrilled to work with newcomers as well as veteran actors equally; they provide a blank canvas, the paint and a willingness to *give* in order to interpret their version of the words in front of them. This is truly rewarding. No matter what the result, artistic moments can happen spontaneously without advance warning and can become amazing experiences.

Jeff's notebook

These boxes are little tid-bits of thought shared from my own personal experiences. They are scattered throughout the book and hope to offer some hints and suggestions so that you can "Take away" some mistakes and discoveries I have made.

While we may be selling soap with our voice-overs, the process is just as detailed, precise and creative as an actor preparing for Hamlet. No kidding. The only difference is that soap is sometimes more fun to work with.

Under No Uncertain Terms

Terminology was never a favorite learning methodology for me either. I always found it frustrating to ascribe meaning to words without a practical understanding or actual usage in my vocabulary. Do you say, "quixotic" on a regular basis? Neither do I. The best way to incorporate this new vernacular is to begin using it in context within the professional environment that asks for it. So here are some words and their meaning that we use regularly in the VO world. Some may be obvious, while others may surprise you.

Call to action   A technique used in commercials to motivate the listener/viewer to "do" or respond in some active way. "Call now!", "Hurry" "Wait", "Find out more", "Go to www.action.com", etc.

Breathy   A vocal quality that is sometimes used to imply secretive intentions. It is also used as a sexy vocal characterization.

Cans   AKA headphones. They go over the ears so you can monitor yourself while recording. This often "throws off" the performer when first using them because it sounds so bright or hyper-real. Actors should get used to the sound of their own voice as quickly as possible. We all have a negative reaction to our voices because our brains cannot seem to reconcile the difference between how we sound everyday, which is pre-conditioned, to how we sound when we are recorded. Our brain's listening center is different than our speaking center, thus the confusion and negative reaction to our voice. It's universal that we all have this "Ugh…do I sound like that?!" reaction.

Copy   This is the script the performer uses. The copywriter is the person responsible for writing it. Simple enough.

Dub   Many voice-over performers are hired to "replace" a voice that is filmed or already shot. Frequently the extremely attractive model with the perfect body may be saying, "It's better than…you know" on camera but, more often than not, the voice is *not* coming from the model, but from a voice-over actor that has a vocal quality better suited to the product's concept. Lip syncing is really what is being done.

Falsetto   Thin, shrill voice placed high in pitch and has a forced quality.

Levels   This term is often used by engineers to achieve the correct recording volume. "Give us a level" simply means to start reading the script so that the adjustment can be made for optimum recording. It is important to perform the script as if it were the actual audition, with proper inflection, tone and attack so that you can represent yourself properly when recording is underway.

Gain   A technical term used by engineers when volume modulation is in need of adjustment. Also known as *riding the gain.*

Looping   When shooting a film, there are times when the vocal sound quality is poor or does not provide the clarity needed for emphasis. Other times, commercial films that contain swear words will not be considered for network television broadcast unless these no no's are looped or reworded by the actor. Looping is the post production recording of dialog by an actor (usually the one who played the part) to suit the demands of the production.

Mic
Short for microphone. This is the electronic device which records your voice. While there are several types of mics used for voice-over applications, most are called condenser microphones. Often the brand name is substituted for the generic term. Different mics offer different results when recording.

Mix
Adding additional production elements to the recording. Like a cake, it is a combination of ingredients to create the "mix".

Nasality
"Speaking through your nose". Usually, an unpleasant speech quality in which the voice is placed through the nasal passages, resulting in an unusual *pinched* or *hollow* sound.

Pace
Primarily a function of time, pace is the overall length of time to complete a word or phrase. A common issue for newcomers is a fast pace. In other words, sounding as if you are in a race to the finish line (end of the copy). Pace can also be a function of mood, character and emphasis and is often confused with energy. They are two separate concepts (more on this later).

Pause
Also a function of time, the pause is the space between words or thoughts. Sometimes called a "Beat" by actors, the pause can be a most useful tool for both internal and external methods of copy interpretation.

Pickup
During recording, it may become necessary to re-do (re-record) a section from a specific point in the script. This is a pickup. The talent must retain the same performance energy and intention when this occurs so that it sounds seamless to the listener.

Pitch
Used in musical terminology, it applies to acting as well. The pitch is the vocal "note" if you will, of your voice. This can be an extremely valuable tool for speaking the copy in many ways. We usually talk in pitches that are most comfortable for us in everyday usage but can shift or change when we are nervous, excited, angry or sad. Changing the pitch in your delivery can convey a variety of emotions and expressive interpretations of the script.

Pot
Not what you're thinking. Short for potentiometer, it is the control room device used when changing volume levels.

Production
When used in voice work, it is the additional manipulation of the recording which may or may not include music *beds* (under the VO, get it?), sound effects (SFX), ambient sound (background) or other elements that contribute to a finished project.

Promo
A specific category of voice-over found on cable networks, and tv stations that is often associated with station identification, upcoming programs, network tag lines (repeated catch phrases). "This is CNN" is one memorable example.

Que
Actors are familiar with this term because it sometimes means, talk sooner, or "Pick up your Q's!". In VO work, it has several different connotations. 1) It is used as a starting flag when voicing live announce or narration work. The director may say "Que announce", which simply means start talking. 2) A que is also used when working with another actor/announcer on the same project. You may hear the last few words or phrases from another actor, whereupon, you are expected to perform your line in full performance mode. This is sometimes called a pickup.

Slate
Taken from the film industry, a slate is a marker reference point used by the audio technician and/or the sound producer to establish an identification name with the performance. It is the way of simply attaching your name to your voice. Usually, "Hi, I'm name is (insert your name here) Take 1" or sometimes your agent's name is asked for as well. I will discuss this in more detail later.

Spot
The commercial itself; short for the entire finished project.

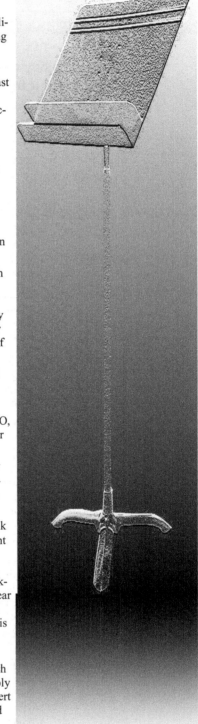

Storyboard	Often used for on camera commercial auditions, a storyboard is a pictorial representation of the entire "spot". Usually roughly drawn like a cartoon, it lays out each shot in sequence on one side of the page, while the other side describes the action and dialogue, including the VO or Announcer.
Subtext	Actors use this "method" technique all the time. It is also quite useful when interpreting the copy. It is applying an inner dialogue or response to the line or phrase that is written. In other words, "I love you" can sound completely different when your subtext is, "*I can't stand you*". Or while smelling the coffee, you are thinking, "*This is going to taste delicious*".
Throaty	A forced vocal quality that is also called guttural. It conveys coarseness, crudity. Used appropriately, this can add unique dimension to a character.
Tremulous	A speaking pattern that has a forced and inconsistent "wavy" quality.
Wrap	As in, "That's a wrap" meaning we're done!

While this is in no way a complete list of voice actor *lingo*, it is more than enough for you to feel confident when you audition or book your first recording session **and** hear it being used.

Jeffrey Dreisbach in a studio recording session with a voice-over actor

Jeff's Notebook

Throughout this book you will find **Workbook Workout** pages. Feel free to copy these pages so that you can have multiple options for each exercise to practice with.

Exercise:

On the next page you will find a media checklist. In it are different voice-over examples that we are exposed to. By keeping this checklist handy and filling out the information as it occurs, you will soon discover the many opportunities there are for VO work. By listing the time, product or service and persona (kind of voice presentation; ie. narrator, real person, character) you should begin to develop a realistic understanding of the methods and approaches being used. Keep your choices focused on performances that sound right for you. In other words, what you might be cast in or that **you** could perform.

Workshop Workout

Voice-over media checklist

Complete the checkbox as it happens in your normal day to day experiences. Provide as much detail as you can about the performance style, persona, and product category of the voice. Add as many types and styles to this list as you can that are right for you. Are there other examples you can add?

☑	DATE TIME	PRODUCT/ SERVICE	MEDIA	CHARACTER STYLE/PERSONA OR CATEGORY
			Phone messaging	
			Website voice	
			Radio	
			TV Commercial	
			Live	
			Toys/Games	
			Audio Books	
			Narration (recorded)	
			Film Looping/dub	
			TV or Cable Promo (station promotional announcement or station promotion)	
			Film Trailer	
			Other	
			Other	

Commercial Copywriters and Their Copy

You may be wondering "why do I need to learn about copy writing?" After all, it is someone else's job to write the commercials, narration, promos! This is true. The copywriter (when talking commercials) works for the advertising agency, radio station, TV station, cable company, newspaper or magazine. Their job is to write an effective commercial that gets the job done, namely, influence the customer to buy the goods or services being written about. The best copy (script) contains several techniques that the writer uses to accomplish this. It can be extremely important when doing voice-over work because they contain keys to interpreting the intention and therefore, influence the performance dynamics and choices when voicing the spot. So here are some common, basic rules the writer might consider when putting pen to paper. Understanding their purpose can save you a lot of time and frustration because you don't have to guess *why* something is written the way it is.

You are now a professional copywriter…(put yourself in their shoes, it will increase your copy appreciation!). First, your rules are:

Get attention "Hey!, OK! Oh No…!"
Hold attention "Your wait is over, Introducing…, It's…"
Build interest "But wait, there's more…Unbelievably low price"
Create desire "While they last, Guaranteed, Money Back…"
Get action "Act now, Just call, What are you waiting for?!"

Many methods are used to apply these rules by the copywriter. Here are some common elements to think about when you are writing the perfect commercial.

- *Use attention getters*: Music, sound effects and character voices all help to add interest to your copy.

- *Know your audience*: Who you are selling to can affect your vernacular and vocabulary choices. This is called demographic targeting…A teenager would probably not sell adult scooters.

- *Keep it simple and to the point*: Stay away from vocabulary that tries to impress the listener. Be clear and concise, overused adjectives are a common mistake amateurs make.

- *Sell early*: Present the goods or services sooner rather than later. You have limited time to make your case. You run the risk of losing my interest if I'm not sure what you are promoting.

- *Write for the ear*: Being conversational is often useful when writing for specific products. "Keep it real" is the phrase most often heard from directors. Unless you are writing an outrageous character spot, it's best to use everyday vernacular...ya know...common, natural sounding speech.

- *Copy preparation*: Think about your commercial's approach to presenting the concept. Write out (phonetically) any words that may be difficult to say. Underline any words that might need specific emphasis. Commas, exclamation points, dot dot dot...can help.

- *Use positive action words*: Sometimes referred to as "Call to action", action words literally compel the listener to act. "Today", "Hurry in", "Call now" and the famous, "Wait, there's more!" Each is designed to motivate the respondent to *do* the action, namely get into the mode of actually buying the product or service.

- *Put the listener in the picture*: Called "theater of the mind", good copy puts the audience in the picture you are painting. It's not enough to talk about the burger, you must involve the listener by letting them experience the taste, aroma, and wellbeing associated with food or whatever you are writing about.

- *Mention the product often*: Repeating the 800 number, product name, physical location or how to get more information is reaffirming product retention. We should remember the commercial long after it is over.

- *Be creative*: The best results for effective commercials are ones with which the receiver has been rewarded for their time. By this I mean the viewer has either been entertained, educated, moved or affected emotionally to the experience. Just "selling" without the added value of connected experience is simply taking advantage of the audience.

Jeff's notebook

Sometimes, students have a very hard time understanding commercial script writing. I am always surprised by this. Given the amount of time we have been subjected to various commercials, promotional advertisements and media in general, being able to recall examples should not be a such painful experience.

Understanding the copy components is useful so that we can explore the variety of styles and delivery techniques available to us. This will help you shift from writer comprehension to performance perfection...I love alliteration, sorry!

There are, of course, specific writing formulas that can help the actor ensure a successful delivery. At least one of the following principles is found in almost all VO copy. When identified, it can help us see how the writing directly influences an audience and assists our performance choices. After reading this section, see if you can identify any/all of these "tools", especially when used effectively on TV or radio:

- *Problem/Solution:* Sore, watery eyes? Itchy feet? Hungry? Tired of waiting? These rhetorical questions are presented for just one purpose, to create and engage the listener with a problem. I've never met anyone who actually enjoyed itchy feet, have you? Sometimes these "problems" are subtle but the effect is just the same; you have a situation that needs to be fixed, solved or answered. What makes this such a successful technique is that within seconds, you can provide the answer and solve the problem. "It's the solution you need!" Simply use the product or service and your problems are over. Eye drops, foot powder, food, express lanes etc., will make your life easier, worry-free, and become the answer you were looking for. For the writer, it is important to recognize two essential facts:

1. Problem = bad: You need to present an emotional scenario by letting the audience realize *how* this affects you (the character or persona) and therefore, affects the audience (who you are speaking to).

2. Solution = good: The result that you feel or experience by using the product/service needs to be expressed so that your audience can respond to the solution in a positive way.

Often, an effective method for transmitting the Problem/Solution is to relate personally to the situation. If you have ever had to wait in line, you know how aggravating it can sometimes be. Your own past experience can influence your presentation of the problem. Conversely, when the solution made you feel better, expressing your emotionality can leave a lasting impression.

- *Contrast/Compare:* "Better than the other leading brand". You might hear this writing element commonly used when household products or new cars are being sold. The method of delivery may be different but the point is the same. That is, the product/service being sold is just as good as, or better, than what you may already know. Additionally, the advertisement may go further by pointing to several reasons why it is

15

better to buy brand "X" over brand "Y". A clear understanding of what contrasting/comparing can accomplish is an important component for the copywriter when writing the spot. The interpretation you choose can have differing effects depending on the choices. It can have a clinical-sounding edge, while other choices might include a humorous point of view when comparing the products. Being clear about the choices depends on the writer's perspective and products' campaign strategy.

• *Information/Motivation:* Sometimes the advertisement may be strictly a listing of information about the goods or services being sold. This type of commercial is often a challenge because the copywriter might not have a purpose in mind other than a "Call to action". That is, to motivate the respondent to accept the information and then act upon it. (See vocabulary section re *Call to action*) Other times, it's called a "soft sell", but it does not mean the writer has a passive voice and only provides the information. It means that the method can be more subtle and may be written in such a way that the actor is required to infuse the spot with energy, enthusiasm, and conviction. It, really depends on *who* is presenting the information that connects the audience to the product or service.

• *Humor:* Believe it or not, humor is subjective for commercials. It is often a challenge for the copywriter to make it funny. We might have a tough time getting the joke if we are not sure we are hearing a joke. Putting aside character, humor in the writing means that you must first get the joke and then be sure it is successful for your audience. If it isn't funny to you, chances are it will not be funny to your audience. Is the punch line funny when delivered by anyone, or is it funny because of who is telling it? Knowing these distinctions can provide you with clarity with which can embellish the copy appropriately. By comprehending the humor as written, the performer will be more likely to interpret the script with performance choices that are successful. Writing a "character" becomes a useful and separate tool for copywriters. The actor is, therefore, the "decoder" of *what* is funny and *who* is making it funny and needs to understand the distinction between them.

• *Mood:* Sometimes the overall mood in the script can be especially important. Adjectives that are often used include: sexy, scary, clinical, funny, sad, emotional, uplifting, romantic, dangerous…

Exercise:
Now that you have been shown how to be a copywriter, it's time to write. Create a :60 commercial voice-over using a real product or service. Use two or more of the copywriter's steps. This is the best way to experience what it takes to put a "Spot" (commercial script) together. You may choose to use this commercial in the next exercise so don't ignore the benefit of this step. Next, perform your script out loud, as if you were in a class of VO students.

The very first thing I do when I receive a script is read it to myself several times. Believe or not, I had to learn this. My previous method was to *conjure up* a character and start immediately "sounding" like the character I thought might work. I did this hoping that the immediate choices I made would be good ones for the commercial. Wow, what a way to miss out (especially during an audition). I always felt rushed to digest the copy rather than comprehend it first. I now take my time, read it to myself, making sure I answer several important questions like: 1) Who is speaking? 2) What is being sold? 3) What copywriting methods are being used? 4) What tools in my writer's "Tool Kit" would serve the spot best? Since this is also vital to the actor's method of working, let's explore each one of these questions individually:

Who is speaking? The answer can be broken down into four basic categories: *Spokesperson/Announcer, Character, Real person, Narrator.*

• ***Spokesperson/Announcer:*** This is typically a personality whose job is merely to present the product/service. Often, the actor has an "everyman/everywoman" quality that is relatable to their audience. Usually, there is a very "straight" style of copy delivery that is intended to tell the audience about the factual, informational elements without trying to draw attention to themselves. Announcers are the original spokesperson persona. In the past, the announcer was typically male with a deep, rich-sounding voice and commanding personality. We were comforted by the sound of their voice. They sounded trustworthy. Today, the market has expanded to include women. They might be the retail voice announcing the "Red Tag" special, or the car spokesperson with a contrast/compare or call to action message.

• ***Character:*** A character is usually written to attract the buyer not only to the product but to make a connection to *who* is delivering the message. Characters are typically actors because they can deliver a realistic connection to the script. It is a partnership between the product AND the personality. If the audiences can relate, and then react to the commercial voice-over artist, then the product is associated with that persona and vice versa. The challenge for some actors is to explore how big or how small to present the character they are playing.

(Continued on page 19)

Exercise:
On the following page, there are exercises for you to perform. This will help you utilize the various commercial copywriter tools and provide first hand experience for creating your own effective commercials. (Use the last assignment if you like or, better yet, write a new one!) Now read the "spot" as if you are in an advertising agency pitch meeting as you might imagine it. Record it if you like, although it is not imperative that you do so. Imagine yourself in a studio as you "show" your commercial idea to agency honchos. The point is to see if the writing tools work well for the concept. Actor interpretation and performance choices should logically follow your writing concepts.

Workshop Workout

Copywriter Challenge

1: Write a :60 commercial on any product or service. It must be a real thing, not made up. Be sure to use the 5 rules and have fun! (Just in case you did not do the last exercise...I know who you are!).

2: Using this commercial, cut (edit) the spot down to :30 seconds. Keep as much of the original "flavor" of the :60 commercial, only shorter.

3: Now reduce the commercial to :15 spot, keeping the most important information in the commercial. Keeping only the essential information in the spot will expose the importance of word economy and performance objective.

:05

:10

:15

:30

:45

:60

Therefore, since brevity is the soul of wit,

And tediousness the limbs and outward flourishes,

I will be brief.

Hamlet

Sometimes being "over the top" is called for, while other times a more subtle choice may be appropriate. Character choices are left for the actor to make using creativity, good taste and judgment with respect to the copywriter's intentions and choices.

- ***Real person:*** is really that. A trend in voice acting today is to sound real. That is, not a spokesperson or a character but someone who seems to have zero performance skills and is not presentational in any way. You may think that when you hear such a spot it is just a real person (not an actor). This is often not the case. Actors are used because of their unique ability to sound conversational, meaningful and genuine. They are also used because they are comfortable sounding that way in a studio environment or on a street (with the noise of traffic, people, restaurant sound, etc.) in the background (also known as ambient noise). For many performers, this is quite difficult to achieve because it requires the ability to completely remove their acting technique; something that may have taken years to develop and grow. It's not easy being real for some of us!

- ***Narrator:*** is in essence, a storyteller. While the narrator's personality is similar to a cross between an announcer and a real person, the narrator must maintain an "in the moment" presence. The reading skill level is most important as the copy can be a book or longer script, such as a film or television documentary. Often, it is the exceptional sounding voice that is warm, sincere, empathetic or authoritative that is cast.

Answering a few additional basic questions can eliminate much uncertainty when it comes to the VO script. These various elements can form a great foundation for you from the outset. We will now slowly move away from being a writer to being a voice actor. What you will get out of these elements is a systematic approach whether writing or performing a script.

What is being sold or told? This may seem like an obvious requirement for good commercial voice-over interpretation. In narration work, what story is being told? Simple, right? In reality, though, I have worked with actors who can't tell me what is being sold or told after a VO narration performance! Equally, the commercial can have an unclear message or one that is purposefully cryptic, to create an atmospheric intention. Knowing what is being sold/told goes to the heart of choices an actor makes for good copy interpretation. You would not have a high energy delivery when discussing a funeral home. You should not sound like an axe murderer and "pitch" The Hallmark Channel. Also, consider that sometimes it is not a product that is a hard sell but rather a series of impressions being articulated by the actor. "Yum", "Share the fantasy", "I love you, etc.". It is your job to make the best choices based on what's being sold and what the story is really about.

What writing methods are being used? If you need to, please re-read the prior section on copywriter tools. By having a clear understanding of what the writer intended, you are able to make discriminating decisions on how to perform it. For example, if you have copy that reads, "I have a headache this big...I took Excedrin, and now I feel better", you can clearly identify this as a problem/solution example. You might use the first part of the copy to portray that you are having an actual headache. The next section, you are taking the product, you might now sound hopeful. Finally, "I feel better" is you, happy to be free from pain. Knowledge of the writer's methods can provide endless opportunities for making choices that connect to the audience.

In the past? Or right now? Notice that the line in the above example reads, "I *have* a headache this big"...not "I *had* a headache this big". One is an active choice while the other is relating to a past headache event. An active choice is usually better because it puts the actor in an immediate time frame rather than something that happened before (past tense).

What, if any is the emotional attachment? "Our toothpaste stays fresher, longer than the other leading brand!". How does the VO actor *feel* about our toothpaste? Excited? Happy to be sharing this fact? Conversely, how does the actor feel about the other leading brand? No matter how broad or subtle your delivery, the script is providing hints on how to transmit your emotional vocabulary so that we (the audience) get the point. Keeping a sharp eye on these copy clues will creatively convey the intended meaning for the actor to interpret.

We can now shift our focus toward the performer's vocabulary. While we keep in mind all of the opportunities the writer has provided, the actor has the responsibility for making them come alive. Breathe life into the words, resuscitate the meaning, jump start the script, reach into the abyss, conjure up a character....ok....I'm done now...

Hamlet: Suit the action to the word, the word to the action, with this special observance, that you o'erstep not the modesty of nature:
Hamlet

Interpretation Tactics

- *What persona serves the copy best?:* Thinking in terms of persona has helped me take my time and focus on the personality the script contains and then decide which options are best for performing. You can easily do this by first seeing *how* the copy is being presented. Are there keywords to act as a guide for the level of energy needed? What type of energy is being asked for? Do not confuse your persona's pace with energy. Pace is a product of character timing while energy is a product of drive and intensity.

- *Transformation:* How does the character change as a result of either using the product or sharing information about the product? I might change from boring to brilliant or scary to funny within the :30 second spot. I might become more satisfied or even smug by the time the commercial is over. Transformation is not necessarily a tool for narration. Narrators need to see themselves as impartial observers while telling the story. That is not to say they cannot "suggest" character within the story. It's just that the narrator should *refrain* from emotional transformation while telling the story.

- *Drive:* What is the underlying force that moves the script along. In other words, how are you sharing this information? Similar to energy, drive is the "I can't wait to share this with you" subtext (inner dialogue of the character) that infuses interest and purposefulness to the script.

- *Personalized:* To whom are you speaking? Imagine all the various interpretations that can occur if you are addressing someone special. If you have clearly defined your listener, then the script will have a significant and compelling quality. By speaking to "the general public" (unless specifically asked for) you are *broadcasting* the message while personalized choices help listeners feel *individually* spoken to. More often than not speaking to one person provides the best script interpretation.

- *Name of the product:* (commercials and promos only) Always point out (verbally, that is) and highlight the product name. You can do this several ways: Take a beat before the name, slow the pace while saying the name, adjust the pitch of your voice when saying the product, change your emotional state when you say the name, (try smiling when you say the name). All of these can be effective uses of letting the listener know what is most important…the product or service you are promoting.

- *Gear Shift:* If you have ever driven a stick shift car then you know how to perform this important driving function. You must first push in the clutch, shift the gear, then slowly let out the clutch to engage the transmission while maintaining a smooth transition into the gear. Gear changes can be fantastic tools for voice-over work as well. The reason they work so well is that they can increase interest by "shifting" the delivery and thereby compel the listener to pay attention. The way in which a successful gear change can work is by breaking it down into four specific components that happen to begin with the letter "P":

1. Pitch: By ending one thought on a "note" then shifting the next thought on a different (higher or lower) vocal note, you will infuse both thoughts with dynamic performance energy. Example: "I like New York in June (shift) **how about you?"** So instead of keeping the sentence as one continuous note, you now divide the thoughts by giving the second half a *shift* by changing pitch.

2. Pace: When you separate the sentence into two separate elements, then shift by increasing or decreasing the rate at which you speak, interesting emphasis is achieved. Example: (fast) "I like New York in June (shift slower) h o w   a b o u t   y o u ? " The question is now more interesting, provocative and perhaps even more fun when you "change up" the pace.

3. Pause: This is an excellent device for creating interest in the copy. Finding the right moment to pause can emphasize the copy for dramatic, comic or chilling effect. Example: "I like New York in June (shift Pause/beat) ...**how about you?"** Notice that I use the word beat here. A beat is much the same as a pause but there are some differences as well. Even though the beat is silent, there is still a driving energy that is sustained by the performer. That is, not simply a silent moment but more like holding your breath silently. It provides forward movement to the script. Actors are used to the term beat because of this implied function of energy.

4. Punctuation: Often the shift of intention can occur through the use of punctuation. A period, comma, and/or dots and dashes can imply a new approach or verbal attack. Make sure you explore the range of possibilities and how these symbols work for you. It is sometimes helpful to literally read the punctuation out loud, as part of the scripted dialogue. In this way you will be compelled to initiate a gear shift for every punctuation mark. Remember that the exclamation point or period, for example, is there for a reason. Incorporating their usage will enhance your performance skills. Example: "I like New York in June ...(ellipse) how about you?!" (question/exclamatory)

- ***Character traits:*** If you are playing a character, perhaps there are certain traits or affectations that may be used in order to elevate the humor or add credibility to the copy. If you have discovered that the scripted material you are voicing is a character (not an announcer), now is the time to decide how the character should sound. This is the creative decision you need to make unless you are told specifically what is being sought. This can range from an accent to a slobbering "s". Perhaps the voice is pitched higher or lower to add more personality to the character you are playing. Perhaps the copy is better served if you use a monotone voice. If you are playing an animated character, clearly your image of the way the character looks will affect the way the character will sound. On the other hand, it may be important to be conversational, natural and re-alistic in your delivery. You may be playing an expecting mother talking about what being pregnant feels like. The tone and quality of speaking as if only to a close personal friend may be the best choice. How would you sound if you were saying "I love you" to one person as opposed to a crowd? Seeking the right voice can be a fun process, yet many times I see problems with choices actors make when developing a character trait. It mostly has to do with commitment.

Many times the performer doesn't believe who they are playing. It sounds fake, phony and uncommitted to the reality that is being created. Unless you can invest yourself fully and completely into a character trait, perhaps it is best to not make that choice. *You* must first embrace the choices before others can.

Subtext is another important character trait. What you are thinking while performing the material can color the choices you make as well. Are you happy to be sharing this information to an audience? Are you in love? Are you really angry when you say "I hate housework!" or are you just trying to make a point? Both can be valid choices. Using subtext can add richness and additional color to the script.

It may be important to bring up character traits that are spontaneous. Adding quirky elements to the script can provide uniqueness to the character. You have an obligation to be letter perfect when you perform the copy but there is (sometimes) room for embellishment. A giggle, laugh or sigh might work for certain characters. If the actor is truthful to the character, adding these subtle quirks can complement the portrayal. What doesn't work is when the actor decides to make subtle choices that are arbitrary or disconnected from the main objective. In other words, are you serving the intension being asked for?

Commercial Scripting

At this point, we need to put into practice our understanding of what a good commercial should look and sound like. On the next page you will find a common layout often used in commercial work. The top of the page contains information typically found in an advertising agency's script. It is helpful to the actor as it may be the actual audition script. The main body of the page consists of two primary elements. On the left side is the storyboard. It is a written or visual depiction of the commercial. For TV commercials, it will often contain frame by frame camera shots drawn (sometimes crudely) like a cartoon. For radio spots, the music, sound effects (SFX), and ambient sound may be described using notation in the information section of the script. On the right side of the page is the dialogue and voice script. What is being said corresponds to the graphic representation on the left side. The *time code* is written in to give a general sense of the length of the copy in relation to the action.

During my workshops, I redistribute these completed spots to each actor so that they have an unfamiliar commercial to audition with. It is also a positive and unique experience to hear how someone else interprets your words. You will, hopefully, understand exactly what a copywriter has to go through. This may also reveal a new respect and appreciation for the writing process. You will never hear me say, "who wrote this s#!*t". I am simply the interpreter to someone else's words...I am not in a position to critique or criticize, but to perform.

He would drown the stage with tears,

And cleave the general ear with horrid speech,

Make mad the guilty, and appall the free,

Confound the ignorant, and amaze indeed

The very faculties of eyes and ears.

  Hamlet

Exercise:

Write a :30 second commercial in the space provided on the next page using what you have learned to this point. If you choose to write a TV ad, then use the screen shot boxes to draw each scene. Have fun. The only rule is that you must write about a real product or service. Cast yourself in whatever capacity you think will show off your best vocal assets. You may want to copy this page and write more than one.

Workshop Workout

Radio/TV spot Storyboard with Script

Time: :30   ☐ TV   ☐ Radio   ☐ Other media _____
Name of product:_____Author:_____
Production notes: _____

Music/Storyboard graphic/SFX	:00 VO:
Music/Storyboard graphic/SFX	:05
Music/Storyboard graphic/SFX	:10
Music/Storyboard graphic/SFX	:15
Music/Storyboard graphic/SFX	:20
Music/Storyboard graphic/SFX	:25
Music/Storyboard graphic/SFX	:30

Now that we have dissected some of the script components and actor choices, it is time to assemble these ingredients and make a *voice-over soufflé*. If we can selectively employ the techniques and intentions that the script is asking for, we are ready to put it all together, mix it up and rise to the occasion. I am so sorry you had to read that last sentence.

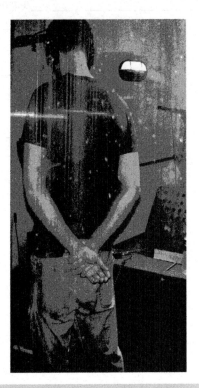

VO student Enrique Gonzalez in a voice-over recording session

Exercise

*Take time to read each of the following liners (brief commercial or promotional scripts) on the next page and fully explore the variety of choices available based on their components (broken down on page 28). Treat this as an audition preparation session and exploration of copy interpretation. You should be able to start exercising the "muscle" of choice and commitment. Each liner should meet the basic qualification we have learned, copywriter driven or character driven? Clear understanding that both are important when you rehearse these. Please remember to have fun. If we take this kind of work too seriously we risk the trap of loosing our perspective.. That is, it becomes so important, so intense, that we sometimes forget we are performers selling toilet paper, cars and happiness. At the same time, it is equally useful to fully perform each spot. By this I mean leave no interpretive stone unturned. Try everything and anything, no matter how absurd, several times before moving on to the next liner. If done correctly, you will quickly discover how much control you have over the material. It will not be in control of you. You will be able to use your voice in ways that can communicate any number of objectives and meet the most important purpose of all, namely, **your** way of selling the product or service.*

Workshop Workout

Voice-over Soufflé

Perform the liners listed below while identifying the copywriting ingredients that are being used. Use the key on the next page to see if your performance choices make sense for each interpretation. Vary the reads as you reveal the various options and VO categories.

1. Wake up to the delicious new taste of FOLGERS EXTRA DARK coffee. Rich, mellow and truly satisfying. Ask for it by name, FOLGERS EXTRA DARK.

2. OK, so just because there are, like, a bazillion choices out there for yogurt, remind yourself that no other brand can out taste new ZOGURT. No one. Not Dannon, not store brands not Yoplait. Nope! And now ZOGURT costs less! Yum...cha ching!

3. When a sinus headache strikes, you need something fast. Try ALEVERT. Proven to be the most effective pain reliever for sinus headache. ALEVERT, you'll feel better...fast.

4. She knows what you are thinking. She can see you in the cool misty light of the moon. She will always find you when you feel lost. Whatever you do, remember her. NIGHT LOVE, the new fragrance for her.

5. I love to run. Really. I feel like the whole world is right there, in front of me. Sure, it's tough but you will never hear me say, "I've had enough". Because passion is what drives me most. NIKE.

6. Find out how Jonathan will pop the question. He's in a boat load of trouble with everyone he works with, not to mention his best friend Cooper. Watch, "OH NO", the hit new comedy, Wednesday's at 8 on ABC Family!

7. It's happening this Thursday. MACY'S one day sale. Take 30% off our entire line of house wares, clothing, specialty items and more... the MACY'S one day sale is this Thursday! Visit WWW.MACYS.COM for special events, prizes and coupons! Macy's one day sale!

8. Whoa cowboy! Just where do you think you're goin'? We're 'bout to tie on the feed bag when all of a sudden, you come out with, "I ain't eatin!" and decide to mosey off somewhere's with nary a "how de do". ANGUS STEAK HOUSE? Well now...I'll saddle up!

Workshop Workout

Voice-over Soufflé breakdown

Use in conjunction with the liners on previous page

1. *1)* Call to action (***Wake up***) *2)* Brand name (***Folgers Extra Dark***) *3)* Descriptive sensual (***rich, mellow, truly satisfying***) *4)* Call to action (***Ask for it by name***) *5)* Repeat brand name (***Folgers Extra Dark***)   **Announcer Voice-over**

2. *1)* Personalizer (***OK***) *2)* Information/brand name (***new Zogurt***) *3)* Contrast/Compare (***No other brand…***) *4)* Personalizer (***nope***) *5)* Action/brand name/information (***now costs less***) *6)* Character humor (***Yum…cha ching***)
   Character Voice-Over spot

3. *1)* Problem (***sinus headache***) *2)* Call to action (***you need something fast***) *3)* Call to action/solution (***Try Alevert***) *4)* Brand name (***Alevert***) *5)* Factual information (***clinically proven***) *6)* Repeat Brand name/Action (***Alevert, you'll feel better fast***)
   Clinical expert Voice-over

4. *1)* Mood (***she knows…***) *2)* Sensual (***Cool, misty light…***) *3)* Call to action (***Whatever you do…***) *4)* Brand Name (***Night Love***) *5)* Informational/action (***new***) *6)* Information (***for her***)   **Affected moody Voice-over**

5. *1)* First person real person driven (***I love to run***) *2)* Problem/solution (***it's tough but…***)   **Real Person-conversational**

6. *1)* Call to action/pique curiosity question/problem (***Find out…trouble...especially***) *2)* Call to action (***Watch***) *3)* brand name (***"Oh No"***) *4)* Information/action (***new hit comedy***) *5)* information/where/when/how. NOTE: This is a programming promotional script. A specific style of delivery is needed.   **Promo Voice-over high energy**

7. 1) Pique curiosity information (***It's happening***) 2) Information (***this Thursday***) 3) Factual (***30% off***) 4) Information (***what is on sale***) 5) Call to action (***visit…***) 6) Repeat brand (***Macy's one day…***) 7) Incentive (***prizes etc.***) 8) Repeat brand name (***Macy's one day…***)   **Retail Voice-over-driving persona**

8. *1)* First person humorous call to action (***Whoa cowboy***) *2)* Direct connection (***you…you…***) *3)* Humor/direct connection (***narry a how de do***) *4)* Brand name (***Angus Steak House***) *5)* Humorous button (***…saddle up!***)   **Animation Voice-over**

Speak the Speech

SPA, or Station Promotional Announcements, are treated as a different class of voice-over. Although they fit easily into the commercial interpretation model, there are some unique differences that should be kept in mind. First, these promotional *liners* reflect the energy and personality of the show being promoted AND the station or network they represent. In other words, they are the **voice** of the entire network, cable company or station. The recent trend is to use actors and not traditional announcers. What this means for you, the actor, is that there is now a completely separate category for "promos". This means we should split each of the categories into the following segments. Each is a separate entity and you would benefit greatly if you think of them as having their own style of delivery with specific qualities:

- **Commercials:** *AVO (announcer voice-over) Real person, character*
- **Promos:** *Relatable Announcer and network/show specific persona*
- **Animation:** *Cartoon, character, affected, energized characterization*
- **Narration:** *Warm, real, empathetic, dramatic energy*
- **Audio book reader:** *Story teller without excessive emotional involvement, suggesting characters rather than acting them*

You may be asking what the Promotional *style* is. Unfortunately there is no clear cut answer. Actors that have a distinct quality to their voice are better suited than, say, a "commercial" sounding performer. There is usually something uniquely identifiable with this type of voice-over. One of the best ways to understand what the challenges are for promotional work is to study cable network station promotions. They *promote* the upcoming program or station ID. "You are watching the Food Network". What qualities does this actor present to their audience? Can you understand why this person was picked for this job?

With the increasing demands for voice-overs on the internet, promotion, animation and narration, be aware that (in larger markets especially) separate talent departments are created to cover each category. When you are assembling your sample demo, you might want to consider separate examples in each of these performance areas. (We will cover demos later in the book). This shift not only applies to the radio and TV stations and networks but to talent representatives as well (Agents). Some of the larger commercial agencies may have several agents covering different segments of the voice industry. Sounds crazy...but it's true. The industry assumption seems to be that you cannot possibly be able to perform in all of these categories. This, obviously, has varying degrees of truth, although being a versatile performer is most definitely advantageous as you define your vocal strengths and assets.

Another performance category that bears understanding is when one actor plays more than one part OR will read with another actor as a partner in an audition or session. They are often called *two handers*. This is common in animation work or in commercials that require a dynamic that depends on a relationship with another actor.. The key to performing a two hander is just like a scene for a play or film: Listen to the other character then respond to the inflection and energy delivered by the other actors' character choice. Effective communication is important for a successful exchange. Clearly, if the copy is conversational, you will need to provide the proper sensibilities and dynamics for this. Humor is sometimes written into the character and might only work if there are specific vocal inflections and qualities you bring to the performance.

Occasionally, one actor will play several parts. This happens in commercials, animation and sometimes, narration (where you are *suggesting* a character). It is common for the production team to record the voices separately, especially if you are playing two or more different personas. In this case, having a one-sided conversation with yourself becomes a technical matter. Sure, it demands your concentration and understanding of the character, plot, and arc (the journey the character takes). It also makes for a better final product. It's next to impossible to switch one voice to another *live* without it sounding fake or amateurish. When the voices are added together in post production, it is easier to make the scene sound real or naturalistic. This is also something to consider for your sample demo (more about this later).

Jeff's notebook

Before I jump into an audition or booking (in the next few chapters), I think about how I will be using my voice. Professionally trained singers and actors know the value of taking care of their, "money maker", but many times I see voice-over performers ignore the actual source of their success, their voice. Voice-over actors are, perhaps the hardest working of all performers. In addition to the mental concentration, performance consistency, and emotional focus that is needed, the physical demands can take their toll as well. Here are some suggestions you might like to consider for keeping yourself in top vocal condition.

- Lots of water: Start on hour before your session. Hydration is important to keep yourself from "dry mouth". Chewing gum is also a quick way of keeping mouth tissues moist.
- Stay away from: Milk products (phlegm), caffeine (diuretic), carbonated beverages (burping), some teas (can dry you out). Best choice: water or water with some lemon.
- Exercise: cardio-vascular conditioning is excellent for keeping your breathing strong and conditioned.
- Nasal passages clear: If you are, in any way, not able to breath _fully_ through your mouth (wheezing) or your nose (audible sounds when inhaling) you must find a way to correct this. Allergy medication, deviated septum surgery, inhalants for asthma, etc. are fixes you cannot ignore.
- The basics: Rest, eating well, not smoking, warm up exercises (vocal and physical)...you know the drill...

The Nerve of Some People

I don't know of any actor or voice actor who does not feel nervous in an audition. In fact, most experienced actors will become concerned when they *don't* have some nervousness. An audition is a stressful time that can rob even a well-prepared actor from giving the best performance possible. It can affect the way you think, the way you sound and the way in which you behave at an audition. How does being nervous affect you? You might get butterflies in the stomach. You might feel your heart pounding inside your chest. Sweaty palms, shaky hands and dry mouth are all symptoms. The intensity of your nervousness can range from mild discomfort to debilitating.

Repeat after me: "Nerves are a good thing"... really! First, they are telling us that whatever is happening, it is important. Why? We may be intent on getting approval. We may feel desperate for the financial reward of a booked audition. Often, we can let our lack of preparation, low self esteem and defeatist (*"why do I even bother"*) inner voices command our attention. Second, it is simply a matter of allowing physiological symptoms to take root and grow. We will, inevitably, suffer an exhausting debate within ourselves during an audition.

There is hope. Understand that nervousness is something that happens to everyone. Next, understand that being apprehensive is a *fight or flight* response inherited from our caveman ancestors. When confronted with some unknown danger, the caveman had two choices to make. "Do I run?" or "Do I fight?" In both cases the body intuitively triggered a series of internal actions to deal with the problem. Blood rushed from the brain and stomach to the muscles in the arms and legs (lightheaded). The heart and breathing rate increased significantly because adrenaline, a hormone secreted by the pituitary gland, was released into the bloodstream (sweaty palms, racing heart). All of the caveman's senses went into high alert. It doesn't really matter whether there was fight or flight, the physical response remained the same.

Today, the audition becomes the contemporary manifestation of this evolutionary mechanism. What I have found out over time is that the worst thing I can do when I am nervous is to try to suppress those feelings. It only increases my sense of losing control. Instead, I acknowledge their existence and accept this as part of the process.

Another issue with nerves that can negatively impact an audition is feeling unprepared. It makes sense that the more rehearsed we are the more confident and secure we feel about the audition. Feeling prepared begins with taking back our loss of control by breathing. (see next page)

Workshop Workout

Nerve Buster Number One: *Controlled Breathing*

The very best way to alleviate the stress and nervousness brought on by an audition or performance (of any kind) is the Square Breathing Exercise. This technique has been an extremely valuable part of my audition process. Slow breathing by inhaling via the nose, holding the full breath then exhaling through the mouth, each on a steady four count is all there is to it. Simply repeat four times. (Do not do more than four repetitions as you may experience lightheadedness or even faint!) See below for a graphic representation of this tool.

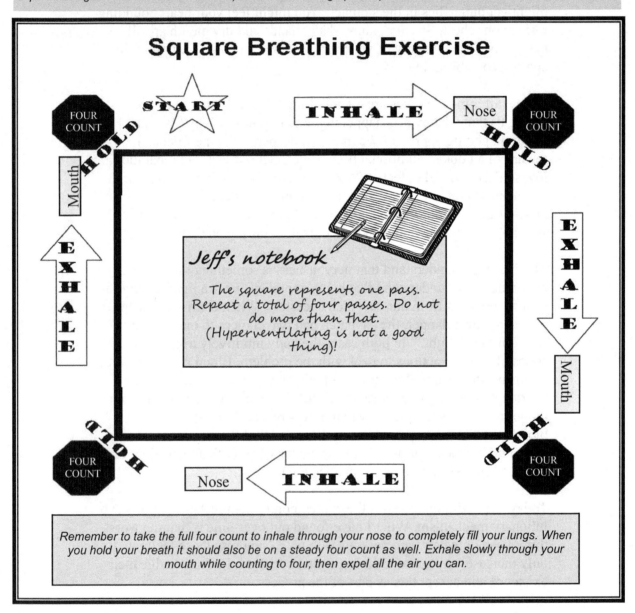

Square Breathing Exercise

Jeff's notebook

The square represents one pass. Repeat a total of four passes. Do not do more than that. (Hyperventilating is not a good thing)!

Remember to take the full four count to inhale through your nose to completely fill your lungs. When you hold your breath it should also be on a steady four count as well. Exhale slowly through your mouth while counting to four, then expel all the air you can.

Once we have taken some control over our runaway nerves with square breathing, continue next with a full vocal warm-up **before** you rehearse the copy.   (see the next page)

Workshop Workout

Nerve buster Number Two: Vocal Warm-up

Use this simple vocal warm-up whenever you need it; before an audition, as a morning ritual, prior to a booking. With continual use and time, you will notice dramatic improvement with your vocal skills and confidence. Make sure you take your time and do not skip any part of this exercise. After you have completed this page, you can now address any number of issues: auditions, copy interpretation, rehearsals, and bookings!

1. Eyes closed relaxed normal breathing for 3 minutes.
2. Square breathing for 4 reps.
3. Inhale, release breath on slow, steady "AH………" until all breath is expelled.
4. Inhale, release breath on slow, steady "AH………" until all breath is expelled.
5. Inhale, release breath on "AH……."(low pitch) to (high pitch), until breath is expelled.
6. Repeat steps 3 through 5 as necessary.
7. Tongue twisters: repeat the following in rapid succession and repeat:

- TIMING TOUGHENS TRICKY THINKING THOUGHTS
- WILD WACKY WIGGLING WHALES WANDER WESTERLY
- AROUND THE RAGGED ROCK THE RUGGY RASCAL RAN
- SENSELESS SYLLABLES ASSAIL SEVERAL SENSES
- LAZILY LOOKING LUSTFULLY ALONG LANKY LADIES
- WHO'S NEW CLUE KNEW BLUE SHOES SOOTHES MOO'S

Whisper the following using over-emphasized articulation. Wide mouth, crisp phonetics, open vowel sounds and logical breath choices:

IT ISN'T A MATTER OF WONDERING WHICH WAY TO TRAVEL WHEN YOU FINALLY DECIDE TO FOLLOW YOUR DREAMS. PERHAPS IT IS A MATTER OF FINALLY ACCEPTING THE CONSEQUENCES OF THE MANY CHOICES AT YOUR DISPOSAL. WHEN YOU GET TO THIS POINT OF UNDERSTANDING, THEN YOU ARE READY TO TAKE THE OPTIONS AVAILABLE AND CREATE A FUTURE OFTEN ASSOCIATED WITH THOSE WHO HAVE FOUND SUCCESS. IN OTHER WORDS, RESPOND TO ALL OF THE OPTIONS UNTIL YOUR HEART HEARS THE HAPPIEST OF RHYTHMS SO THAT YOU ARE ABLE TO ACHIEVE THE SATISFACTION YOU HOPE FOR.

Auditions, Warmed up With Cold Feet

Great! You've warmed up. Your nervousness has dissipated somewhat. What you do next depends on the various situations you, the performer, might find yourself in. Listed here are scenarios that I have experienced and what to do should they happen to you.

Cold reading: What this refers to is being given a script at the last minute with no chance to rehearse it. This is something that is happening less and less because of the ability to email copy to an actor instantly. Nevertheless, there are still those times when last minute changes, fast session requests, communication mixup's and just plain old "not enough time" happen to us. When this happens, take heed and try to be objective about the situation. Desperation is never a good thing. Being anxious because you were not given the chance to become prepared is not a problem, but rather, a situation. First, see if there is a way to get more time before you are asked to read. Often, the person in charge (casting director, agent, producer) will understand the dilemma and give you a reprieve. Second, if you are given more time, use it. That means you must systematically work through every stage of the scripted material within the time frame given you (The next page has these listed in order). Third, if the first two suggestions don't work, let go of the outcome. You will waste a lot of energy and brain cells if you choose to feel victimized by the situation. Technically, being a good reader is enough to make a positive impression. As long as you don't sound like you are reading, then "winging it" may be your only option. I firmly believe that being a good reader is a learned thing and not related to talent. It is a skill. Simple as that. Reading out loud is the best way to develop this ability. (later in this book).

Making the best audition choices: When we have the opportunity to work on a script, many of us are worried that *our* interpretation, among the myriad choices at our disposal, will be wrong. In other words, "what are *they* looking for?" If, as performers, we are supposed to have a versatile repertory of characterizations, then how can we settle on just one interpretation? The real answer is in not asking this question in the first place. If you have taken the proper amount of time with the tools, techniques and preparation, you will instinctively know how to make the script work for you. Literally, it becomes something that is unique. The only mistake you can make is **not** being committed to the choices you have decided upon. This approach maintains a level of insecurity that is fatal to your creative ability. One way to avoid this trap is to refraine from trying to recreate how you are hearing the script in your head when performing. You will never be as good as your imagination when you rehearse your copy internally. Instead, be confident in the knowledge that you have worked on the material in a careful, productive way. Embrace your point of view (without trying to freeze your interpretive choices) and therefore become fully invested in the material when you perform it. Additionally, the strength of your choices, even if they are different than what is asked for, become more impressive than making neutral uncommitted declarations. Many times, a second read is asked for because of your strongly committed first choice. Remember that the audition is the *final* performance opportunity, not the first. At least that is what you need to tell yourself: "I can't wait to show you how I will play this _____ (character, persona, narrator) for the last time!"

Then there are situations completely out of your control. Last minute copy changes, being partnered with someone, being given the wrong part or not feeling well may occur. Although you may hope this never happens to you, chances are, it will. Inevitably, something will happen that is unexpected or unwelcomed. In cases such as this, you can only practice *acceptance*. Whatever happens, happens for a reason that you may or may not understand. You can only do your best given the circumstances or situation. "Live and let live", is a phrase I use. Being angry, frustrated, feeling victimized, overwhelmed or freaked-out only makes it worse. My best advice is to move on. You simply cannot control circumstances that are out of your control. Having a positive mental attitude mixed in with a little humor is sometimes the best strategy when things go wrong.

Now that we have looked at various scenarios that might affect your performance techniques, you can employ a systematic approach for deciding what interpretative choices work best for the material, when you have the time. Like the breathing exercise and vocal warm-up system, using an approach that is laid out in stages increases your confidence and ultimately defines your abilities as an accomplished VO artist.

Jeff's notebook

Remember to eat something before an audition or booking. I have had some embarrassing "outtakes" when an audible stomach growl stops a take. Be mindful of other noises that might draw undue attention to you and not your performance...you know what I mean. Burping, of course!

I have a set of steps, a structure if you will, for every script I work on. I cannot just "rehearse" the copy, I work it *in order*. Here's how you can become perfectly prepared:

- ***Read the copy to yourself:*** Obviously, this is the first step (after square breathing). It is important to read to yourself first with NO imposed character or interpretation. Refrain from performing it in your head. Read it slowly so that it makes perfect sense to you. The *product* you are talking about, each and *every word* that is written, every *punctuation mark*, must be understood. Repeat as necessary.

- ***Read the copy in a whisper:*** This is an excellent way to continue to absorb the material. When you whisper the words several things happen. You will find potential *verbal* pit falls that may be embedded in the script. The *phonaters*, the lips, the teeth and the tongue, get warmed up helping to achieve clear pronunciation of the copy. Additionally, like square breathing, the whisper helps prepare your voice by allowing warm moist air to pass over the vocal cords. Repeat as necessary.

- ***Read the copy out loud:*** Do your best to not give a performance. This step is vital for a few reasons. You'll find the rhythm of the piece, that is, the energy and pace that works well. Next you'll read the punctuation. Not literally, but make sure that a period (.) is a complete beat while a comma (,) is slightly shorter. An exclamation point (!) is there for a specific reason as are the other non-verbal marks. *Hear* them out loud. Underline them if you need to. Repeat as necessary.

- ***Lastly, give a full performance:*** Do not wait until you are in the audition room for this step. The last *act* of the audition is the audition itself. It doesn't matter who might hear you in the waiting room. If needed, find a quiet place and hear yourself perform as if it were the actual audition. By this point, you will have a full and complete understanding of the script and how you should and should not play the part.

The next page contains some do's and don'ts for auditions or even when you get the "gig" (hired to perform).

Jeff's notebook

When I make a mistake in a session it is usually because of my speaking rate or some word or combination of words that trip me up. When that happens to you, simply stop where you are, take a breath, and begin the sentence where the error occurred. Use the same energy and inflection. The engineer will be impressed and you will have saved the take because it is an easy fix.

Workshop Workout

Audition Home Run or Fowled out

Useful tips to keep in mind when you audition or get hired.

DO	DON'T
Arrive early, square breathe, apply cold reading techniques and enjoy the process.	Arrive late, dress sloppily, talk to friends, "wing it".
Enter the room positively, place your copy on the stand, put on cans, don't speak.	Saunter in, try to be, "chatty", blow into the mic, ask questions before starting.
If requested, give a level by performing the *last* few sentences of a script full out.	Say, "Test, Test, 1,2,3,4...I am talking now...into the microphone…"
Slate your name with energy as yourself. (Smile)	Slate in a character or funny voice, depressed, uninterested, casual.
Take a beat (pause) before and after your slate.	Rush into the copy after the slate.
Know the name of the product, who is talking and the mood of the copy.	Mess up the name of the product, sound like you are reading, lack truthful energy.
Take a clear point of view.	Be general and hope they can get the general idea.
Perform your copy while speaking to one specific person.	Announce your copy.
End the copy on an up note (positive, hopeful, optimistic).	Drop your energy before you are finished.
Say, "Would you like it more (pick one) warm, upbeat, character?"	Ask for a re-take, ask, "How's that?... Do you want me to do it again?"

Slate on thin ice?

A slate for voice-overs is the same as meeting someone for the first time, especially when you want to make a good impression. You smile, extend your hand, **say your name clearly** and make a connection. The VO slate is the same. You smile and say your name, "Hi, I'm (your name)". I have seen actors lose out on a booking because of a cold, disinterested, depressed slate. Really! We make a discriminating decision about another person within 15 seconds of meeting them for the first time. How we feel about ourselves when we walk into a room can leave a positive or negative impression on those we meet. If you are looking for proof, consider this scenario. Have you ever been in an elevator by yourself, feeling perfectly fine, when someone else gets on? After a few floors and the other person gets off, have you felt like your energy was drained? It's as if, without saying a word, you were visited by a vampire and had the life force taken from you. Chances are that the energy "given off" by the passenger had a direct effect on you. I am sure you can recall other instances when this has happened you.

A slate is, literally, a verbal identifier for your audition. When the powers that be listen to the recordings on playback, your name becomes the marking point for your audition reads. It is simply an easy way to catalog your session.

I am often surprised when a student has trouble pronouncing their own name in the studio. It's as if this is brand new information. Practice your own name several times then add it to the whole slate. This is critical if you have a long or challenging name. "Hi, I'm (your name)" is a completely acceptable slate. Another technique is to repeat your first name: "Hi, I'm (first name...first/last name!)" Sometimes a take # or agent name is asked for, "Hi, I'm (full name)...take 1!" If this is asked of you, be ready for it. Say it out loud as part of the entire presentation.

Another type of slate that is almost always unsuccessful is when the actor slates *in character*. That is, uses the same voice as the persona in the spot. The actor, in their effort to be clever, decides to *become* the person they are playing. Think about it. If you have an opportunity to show as many colors as possible, wouldn't a natural sounding, upbeat, "*glad to be here*" slate serve your purpose more effectively?

More recently, there is a kind of slate that is odd, yet shows up frequently. That is, a slate where your name ends up like a question, "Hi I'm (first name, first/last name?). The voice pitch goes up at the end. It really should be understood that you know who you are, don't you? Even after correcting a student several times, they revert to this habit. Say your name as a statement of fact with your most confident self and then, smile!

Finally, why is it important to mention something a simple as "slating" your name? In addition to the first impression, the sincere, positive approach and the proper placement of your name, a slate is often disregarded and therefore appears unimportant, incidental and mechanical. Never miss the chance to perform, even something like your saying your name. It's that simple. Oh, and remember to smile. It boosts your energy in a natural positive way.

What happens next is the scripted portion of the audition/performance. But wait...there's more! Remember to take a breath, beat or pause between the slate and the spot. Do not rush this aspect of your audition. The space between your name and the copy is an opportunity to breathe, get into your character, and launch your commercial promo or narration. This is a confident methodology for both you and those who are evaluating

Gloucester:

The trick of that voice I do well remember;

Shylock:

Shall I bend low and in a bondman's key,

With bated breath and whisp'ring humbleness

The Merchant of Venice

Jeff's notebook

The origins of a slate dates back to the early silent film days. A piece of slate was used with chalk to record the film's name, scene number and "take" number just prior to "action!" being shouted by the director. Later, when sound was developed and added, the piece of slate included a moving clapper to record the snap and movement for synchronizing both elements.

Typical voice-over radio commercial audition script

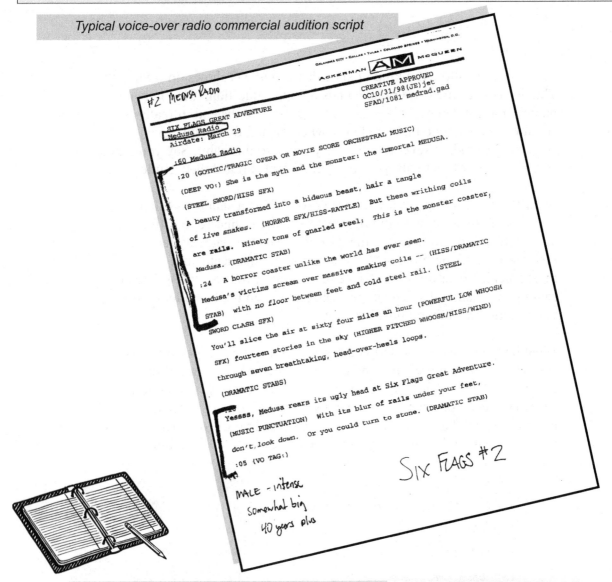

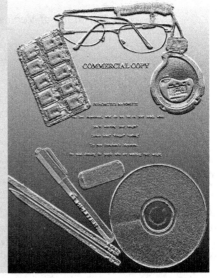

Jeff's notebook

My audition back pack contents:
- ☑ glasses
- ☑ script–(copy)
- ☑ gum
- ☑ stopwatch–(invaluable for timing yourself)
- ☑ 2 pencils
- ☑ eraser
- ☑ highlighter
- ☑ spare VO demo CD
- ☑ 8X10 Photograph–(Shows your professional actor status, just in case)
- ☑ business cards or business brochure

40

Making Your Mark

Marking your audition script with notations presents some cautionary tales of woe. Too much interpretation notation can confuse and remove you from sounding spontaneous and interesting. Additionally, if you must have notes to guide you, consider what may happen if you are asked to perform the copy differently from the way you prepared it. Being committed to your performance AND being willing to make adjustments when called for contribute to the success of a good audition. That said, there are times when making economical notations can, in fact, help you. On the next page are some symbols that I sometimes use when I need to remind myself of specific inflection, timing, pronunciation and punctuation notes that can aid my performance. Use a pencil (or 2) with an eraser. Last minute direction will be easier to adjust if you can remove or replace your notation with changes that may be called for.

Be mindful of the markings already present when you get the copy, that is, the punctuation. The copywriter is actually providing you clues that they believe to be crucial interpretive symbols to use, such as, exclamation points, commas, periods and underlines. I always try to make these notations the *default setting* for my first few reads when preparing any script. Only then will I add my own notation that will help guide my performance choices. I look at *my* notes as another layer to be incorporated into the final "take".

Jeff's Notebook

A warning about making notes when rehearsing the copy. I remember being so obsessed with my symbols: // (pause), ...(Breath), ! (important), __ (product name), * (pronunciation), ↓(pitch down), ↑(pitch up), that by the time I went into the audition, I couldn't decipher any of it. I was completely flummoxed. Use symbols if they help, but be careful when adding too much. It may come back to bite you. By using the steps I have given you, you will most likely remember just about every note you thought of.

Workshop Workout

Notation:	Used for:	Means:
――――― (Underline)	Pronunciation/Take note	This needs special attention
↗ (arrow up)	Inflection	Raise the voice pitch
↘ (arrow down)	Inflection	Lower the voice pitch
// (hash marks)	Timing	Gear change
/ (single slash)	Timing	Pause (breath)
⬭ (circle)	Pronunciation	Potential pitfall
! (exclamation mark)	Punctuation	Stress the point

Adequate preparation and notating the copy means you are ready to audition. The next exercise should test what you have learned so far. Also, by using the right tools to solidify your performance decisions, you are giving yourself a creative "leg up" over your competition.

Exercise:

Using the scripts (liners) on the next page, use your copy interpretation and performance techniques, along with whatever marking system you have chosen to use and "audition". Record yourself and try your best to be objective without being critical on playback. Take your time with each one before moving on to the next. Here are some reminder tips for cold reading:

- *Who is speaking? (AVO-announcer voice over/real person/character?)*

- *What are you selling? (product name).*

- *What mood/energy/approach should you take?*

- *How does the persona change as a result of using or promoting the product?*

- *What kind of copywriter techniques are being used?*

- *Are there any verbal traps or pitfalls?*

- *How should the spot begin? (happy, enthusiastic, sincere?)*

- *How should the spot end?*

42

Workshop Workout

Presenting Liners and Promos

Remember that any audition is similar to a three act play with a beginning, middle and end. Remember to be true to the decisions you make so that you are in the moment.
Think what you are saying...say what you are thinking!

Discover triple protection color. New L'OREAL Excellence Cream. Rich natural color with triple protection AND natural color.

Dove's daily exfoliating bar, with tiny blue beads, gently polishes your skin and conditions it with 1 quarter moisturizing lotion. To reveal fresh beautiful skin every day. New Dove daily polishing exfoliating bar.

Demonstrate your contempt for conformity...3.1 seconds faster. The new Chrysler PT Cruiser turbo. Customize your life.

The ultimate weapon in the fight against gum disease. New Oral-B professional care 7000 series. The most innovative power tooth brush we ever created. Oral B...Brush like a dentist.

Think you know everything about Vitamin C? There are indications that Vitamin C may help reduce the risks of certain forms of cancer. Nature Made Vitamins and minerals, get all the goodness you expect.

Indulge in the soothing ritual of tea. BIGELOW TEA. True joy can actually be found in a cup of tea. Visit www.bigelowtea.com for a free catalog and enjoy classic teas in contemporary flavors.......

Presenting ROLD GOLD Honey Wheat Braided Twists. For the true love of snacking with only 1 gram of fat per serving. Salty and sweet....Rold Gold braided twists.

Sometimes courageous, sometimes outrageous, but always remarkable, witness stories of transformation from people you can relate to. Discovery Health Channel. Real life. Medicine. Miracles.

Trippingly on the Tongue

Now you are, hopefully, feeling more confident about your ability to perform text. Congratulations! There are questions that sometimes arise with actors who may be feeling concerned. It is usually about where they are at this stage of performance growth. It may have to do with a speech issue (whistling "s", lisp, phonic substitutions or other affectation) that will reveal itself after the last workbook workout is recorded. Also, actors with regionalisms (speech patterns based on where they're from), foreign accents, or unusual pathology, may feel increasingly discouraged with the way they sound. So, let me offer some personal advice with issues such as these.

First, if there is some kind of physical condition that precludes you from correct speech production, you must seek help. It's not a matter of sounding bad, but rather, having unnecessary limitations placed on your ability to perform what is requested of you. There are excellent speech therapists who can, in very short order, work with you to correct a variety of conditions and speech issues that affect you. Consider an assessment of your speech at a local college or university with a licensed speech therapist that has experience with actors.

Second, having a regionalism can be somewhat limiting, although less so than with serious speech impediments. Having a deep Southern drawl might possibly work for some voice acting, for example. Hearing the Philadelphia "r" in an audition, could be considered acceptable. However, the vast majority of voice-over work is standard American speech, often associated with the Midwest. If you fall into having a *regionalism*, don't despair. Consider correcting your particular regional sound with standard American speech. It must first be identified, however. There are many speech therapists that can work on this with you. It makes sense; the less regionalism you have in your normal speaking voice, the more work there will be for you.

Third, accents from another country often fall within the same parameters that a regionalism does for the voice-over performer. If you choose not to address this, understand that there may still be opportunities for VO work, only less so. It comes down to a matter of casting requests for your particular accent. Also, a British or Irish accent may be a popular choice, whereas middle European accents may be less called for. It really is a matter of deciding for yourself the kind of voice work you are looking for and the amount of opportunities that exist for your particular issue. If you are bilingual, (meaning you can read and write easily in two or more languages) AND have an American "sound", you would be well advised to market this skill aggressively.

Finally, no two voices are alike. If you have a distinctive voice that is different than the way "normal" people sound, you can promote this uniqueness to your advantage. If your unique quality is off beat, squeaky, sexy, gruff, etc., then you should market your skills for specific casting opportunities. It really is a matter of knowing yourself and knowing what the current casting trends are for your particular trait.

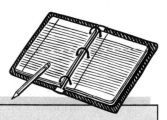

Jeff's notebook

If you have some unique vocal trick, sound or ability, (Sneezing on cue, yodeling, auctioneer rap, singing ability, etc.) it must be part of your resume. List it under "Special Skills". You never know what might be needed and it could land you a job.

Wait, there's even more...

Finding the best "voice" for you to use is a matter of analyzing the various casting categories being asked for *within* the industry. The next few sections address this very subject as we move closer toward some popular categories that should help you select the strongest choices for your voice and talent.

Jaques: All the world's a stage, And all the men and women

merely players;

They have their exits and their entrances,

And one man in his time plays many parts,

His acts being seven ages.

As you like it

William rehearsing his copy in the studio

Actors Real Reel

One challenging request made in voice-over work is when the character is a "real" person. You may be surprised to find out that unless you see or hear a disclaimer such as "actual customer, not an actor" on television, chances are it's an actor. For many actors, this is extremely difficult to do. I am not sure why. After working with many MFA (Master of Fine Arts) students in several workshops, I have made a few observations. The most difficult character to understand, and therefore portray, is the actor as him/herself. There seems to be a disconnect between the person acting and being real. You see, when there is so much emphasis on the process of acting, there leaves little room for connecting internally with oneself. To put it another way, we are much more comfortable when we can play a character than when we play ourselves. Being presentational feels more comfortable but it is also limiting. It limits our ability to fully connect with this style of script. This can apply to commercials, but it can have significant implications on all other categories such as, audio books, film narration and promo's. Often, when I say "just be you" to an actor, what I get is either theatrical or pushed.

The solution to this dilemma is not hard, but does require some work. First, make sure you personalize the copy by speaking to _____ (fill in the blank): lover, girlfriend, boyfriend, spouse, best friend, pet, stuffed animal, etc. It doesn't matter who or what it is, except that it must hold special meaning for you. If you can maintain this imagery during your performance, then your unique relationship is now connected to the script. This is good. Second, talk to your special someone as if they are right next to you. Microphones are amazing things. They can hear you quite well because they are close. Having an intimate sound will infuse your copy with realism.

Third, relax. Yeah, I know, it's not always easy because we have a committed belief that we must be "on" in order to be successful. This is not the case. Imagine talking to your special someone, up close, *without* being relaxed. It is next to impossible, right? Now, try to feel comfortable, safe and at ease with your special someone AND the script. This is where you need to be. Do not confuse relaxation with lack of energy or being intimate with being withdrawn. It is a matter of channeling the energy into the character in a personalized way. Know what you are saying while you are saying it *as* you focus on one person.

Finally, being conversational should be the primary objective for a *real life* interpretation. Simply stated, you cannot *sound* like you are reading.

For some, this can be very difficult to accomplish. Reading out loud on a regular basis helps. Consider the "real" people that you hear in "testimonial" commercials, narration and promotional announcements and you will soon learn the value of having another tool called *real* in your arsenal. Many talent representatives (agents) believe that the more connected you are to the *"real you"*, the more successful your performances are. Being a clearly defined persona with the voice-over script choices you present, will bring more positive reactions at auditions, demos and bookings.

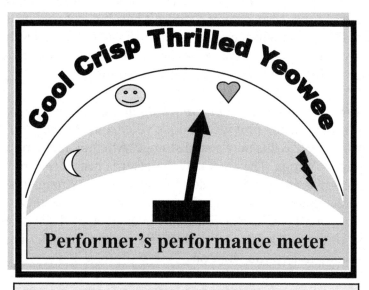

Something to think about...

Rather than thinking about your performance energy levels in literal terms like, faster, louder, and goofy, try processing the energy in emotional terms. Cool, crisp, thrilled, etc. may provide a richer interpretation.

Exercise:

One of the single most important training techniques you can easily do for voice acting is reading out loud. You have the ability for rapid improvement and results by performing this simple task. My recommendation is to read daily for 20 minutes. It doesn't matter what you read, just do it in an easy, conversational manner. After a brief period of time, say, two weeks, you will experience meaningful, tangible results. Additionally, you will start training your eyes and brain to read ahead of what you are saying. This is a good thing because when you read ahead, you are able to comprehend what is happening and therefore, interpret more appropriate inflection choices. In other words, better results with the copy! This is even more critical to those actors wishing to narrate or record books. Typical "Book" reading sessions amount to hours of continuous reading with little or no breaks. This is , therefore, a skill set well worth developing.

Animation Infatuation

J ust as sounding genuine is often a challenge for many actors, animation voicing presents their own set of issues. Many times when, at an audition, a picture or drawing is given out to the actors. This is an effort to assist the talent in developing a corresponding voice for the character they will portray. While it can be fun to experiment with some of your voicing ideas, there are common mistakes that should be avoided. Here are items to consider when taking on an animated character:

- ***Never use a voice that can hurt you in any way:*** Forcing a low, gravelly sound is a potential strain on your vocal cords. Remember that you must be able to sustain that voice in a studio environment over a long period of time. Also, even if it doesn't hurt but if it *sounds* like it hurts, it will ruin your chances for performing. No one wants to be mentally removed from the content by hearing a strained vocalization. The same goes for high, squeaky, forced interpretations.

- ***Make the same commitment you would make as a real person***: I have seen many actors provide a unique voice, but stop short of sounding realistic. I realize this may sound strange. After all, animation is not realistic, right? Wrong. The animated character is just as committed (even more so) as any "real" character. It takes a very strong connection to the characterization to provide the creative dynamics in the *world* they occupy. Don't just have a voice, *be* "in character". The voice is just one aspect of the performance. Invest in treating the character in as detailed a manner as any you work on.

- ***Understand the parameters of the character:*** There are a lot o wacky-sounding cartoons being voiced by very talented folks. Sometimes, the project you are working on might use real-sounding people for their characters. Not all animation uses high-pitched, squeaky, or goofy-sounding characterizations. You will likely get guidelines from the script or other sources prior to your reads. Yet, you must be able to determine what is being asked for and then *deliver*.

Jeff's notebook

During a recording session for an animated spot, the director asked me, "Could you do it again with a bit more energy on the lower notes of the character's inner senses?" I was clueless. Rather than point out his weird communication style, I thought it best to do the spot exactly the same as the previous take. When finished, he beamed, "See, that is so much better!"

- ***Being versatile is often the cornerstone of professional animation acting:*** Switching from one character to another comes easily to the gifted actor. Explore the entire range of characters you have in your arsenal. Make notations about your characters. Read different copy and see if you are able to sustain the character at length. Being consistent with each interpretation becomes a vital component when you are in a recording session.

- ***Never comment on your character:*** Talking about the script when you are off air, making fun of yourself, or just making fun of your character is self-defeating and can diminish your good work.

- ***Always warm up the voice before you start:*** Breathing exercises, tongue twisters, vocal slides, etc. can be your best solution for vocal conditioning. Physical and mental preparedness are key to freeing up your creativity.

- ***Follow direction:*** The creative team, having developed the project, will have definitive ideas as to what approach the actor should take. Listen to them. Taking and following direction and then making it work is your professional responsibility and job description.

Exercise:

What voice would you use for this character? Write out a character description including persona, voice type, energy and mood. Now write a short monologue, record and play back for an objective evaluation.

Jeff's notebook

Use your imagination when you have a picture of the animated character you are to play. I try to never think of what is obvious or cliché. I usually find success in coming up with something unexpected.

Embrace Your Inner Studio

If you take a sheet of paper and draw a line down the middle, the left column could be labeled, "performance". It would include a listing of everything we have covered to this point including copy interpretation, performing techniques, copy decoding and more. The other side of the same sheet could be labeled, "production". This would encompass every-thing technical in the voice-over world. While you may not think that a performer should know technical stuff, rest assured that the information mentioned here can be considered critical to a voice artist. Additionally, some of the production references are useful for the preparation of your demo. The information provided in this section is well worth your under-standing.

When you find yourself in a professional recording studio, understand that there are rules that should be adhered to. Granted, not all recording environments are the same. Some of these guidelines are less important than others. Some engineers, directors, casting directors are not as stringent as others may be. I think it wise to proceed with caution so that you will not feel embarrassed because you were caught unaware.

- ***Do not touch the equipment:*** The headphones are an exception. The rest is usually off limits. Adjusting the microphone, moving the copy stand, turning on lights and re-arranging the furniture are never a good idea. The person in charge of the studio (usually the production engineer) takes great pride and care with the expensive technology. They will usu-ally make the necessary adjustments for you. The headphones or *cans* are fine for you to put on. The volume is adjusted in the control room and can be raised or lowered when it is appropriate to mention. The headphones will serve as a monitor for you. You will hear yourself when the mic is hot (on). Use caution as many of us are surprised to hear ourselves just as the control room hears us. We can be thrown by this. I have seen excellent talent suddenly made self-conscious by this new sen-sation. Also, actors can easily become infatuated with this. They like their voice and start talking for the sheer fun of it. Yikes! To overcome this, it might be a good idea to put one earpiece over one ear and place the other earpiece on the side of your head (behind the opposite ear). In this way you can hear yourself in the room and in one headphone, causing less distraction and undue influence on your senses.

- ***Keep your distance to the microphone:*** I literally make a fist and place it between the wind screen (the round cloth disk in front of the microphone) and my cheek. Once there, I try to stay in this position without excessive movement. I don't want to feel "boxed in" or constrained but it really helps maintain a consistent recording quality.

Also, it keeps me from moving around too much when I am performing. Too much gesticulation really means that I don't know what to do with my energy. It does not impress anyone. My energy should be focused on my script choices first and foremost.

- ***Do not wear the phones around your neck****:* While this may seem like a good idea, feedback because of the proximity of the cans to microphone might occur. Feedback is a harsh, high pitched noise created when the speakers or headphones hear *themselves*, creating what's called a loop. Do not decide to go without the cans, though. The sound booth uses this system to talk to you between takes. Going without will leave you in silence.

- ***Move yourself into position for mic placement:*** The best distance for your mouth to the wind screen (the round cloth disk in front of the mic for deflection air from your breath) should be one *fist* away. I literally make a fist and place it between the screen and my mouth. I do my best to remain in that position for the duration. Granted, I need to feel physically comfortable, but this rule of thumb is a good one. If you are in an audition and then return for a booking or call back, you will appreciate the consistency of mic placement. If you are hired to do extensive recordings, (book reading, for example) the continuity will never be an issue from one day to the next.

- ***Bring two pencils with erasers to every recording session:*** This is part of my routine. I never hold the pencil when I record, I only use them when I am receiving notes or ideas. Excess noise like paper shuffling, kicking the copy stand with my foot, letting the headphone cord touch the mic etc., all of these need to be avoided. Even though it may seem a bit nerve-racking to keep these things in mind, you will ultimately grow confident in the studio over time.

- ***Don't let a recording studio feel odd***: By this, I mean that the room is so devoid of any sound that it can be disconcerting. This is normal. Don't let it throw you. The best recording studios spend significant time and money to achieve this silent effect. Sound deadening is a critical component for optimum recording. Over time I have learned to actually like it. It is the kind of solitary environment that feels safe and therefore, creative.

There are some production facets that may not seem, at first glance, necessary for you to know. Yet, knowing them can help you when you need it. Let's look at a few.

Having a comprehensive understanding of what is involved during a recording session will help you enjoy the project you are working on. As an example, looping refers to recording over an existing performance. It can be your own on camera performance where the script needs adjusting or for better audio quality. You may also be hired to loop another voice with your voice. It can also be a dub or foreign language translation to English. In these cases, you will record a sequence from a raw video or film on a monitor or screen. Your job is to match the voice to the corresponding dialogue. Not always as easy as it sounds. Maintaining your concentration while being free to express yourself *in character* is key. Knowing the parameters of the sequence and being able to replicate the emotional state, energy and pace to match the scene is called for. Don't panic if you find yourself in this situation; it is a learned thing that can be picked up rather quickly. It is also fun.

A two hander refers to two characters in a scene or commercial. In acting classes, *two handers* are often used to explore the relationships, texture, objectives and intensions of the characters. In voice work, two *handers* are frequently used as well. Comic ads for radio and TV often employ this effective device. What is useful in an acting class is also useful in voice-over work. Being able to perform effectively with another actor, therefore, is critical. Usually, it is in a callback (another audition for the same role) that you may be paired with one or more actors in an effort to find the best combination of voices. If this is the case, explore the unique dynamics that exist in a dual scene by trying several interpretive choices. Being a good listener and responsive to the other actor(s) using your best skills make for a good session.

Jeff's notebook

I had to loop myself in *Die Hard with a Vengeance*. The film script and theatrical release heard me say, "Go F#%@ yourself!" This was not going to work for network TV hence, the new line was inserted. I now said, "Up yours yourself!" in the looping session. I'm not sure this made any sense but I was happy to be paid for the day!

Let Music Beds Lie

When you listen to a commercial, animation sequence or other promotional advertisements, there is often a bed involved. Not a bed you sleep in but a music bed. Studio technicians like to *lay down* a bed or track of audio as part of the overall production. It is important to understand the significance of this added ingredient. Knowing the music is a way of comprehending the mood or atmosphere needed for your performance. Even the most subtle music beds are used to influence the respondent's emotions, attitudes and feelings for the goods or services being presented. Among the many ways I like to introduce the value of music in voice-over work is to play "drop the needle" (an old fashioned reference to when records were made of vinyl and phonographs had needles to reproduce the sound). The exercise is easy enough; simply play a recording of any non-vocal music. (Non-vocal is important because we do not want a conflict between what we are saying and lyrics in a recording.) Now, perform any of the commercials we have worked on and see what happens. If you allow yourself to become influenced by the music, your mood, intonation, expression, and overall presentation of the spot will occur. Now, try a different piece of music, perhaps a classical violin solo, and perform the SAME commercial. What happens? Can you make the commercial work with this new music? Sometimes it can really have a powerful influence on our reads, other times it is completely wrong, even comical.

Many times we are able to express ourselves effectively when it is connected to the music being used. We are able to create the atmosphere in seconds with an appropriate bed. When you are listening to commercials, whether on the television or radio (I do hope you are watching tons of TV and listening to radio promos!) pay close attention to this functional device as this is a useful tool for demo sample preparation as well.

Finally, make note of the voice to the music *together*. Levels that are *too hot* (music too loud) have us listening to the music rather than the voice actor, while beds that are *too low* (quiet) may not contribute whatsoever to the spot's intended purpose. The other interesting audio technique that is used is what I call *naked*. That is, no background sound or music at all. This is often used in PSA's (public service announcements) or copy that is meant to elicit an emotional response from the listener/viewer.

When we listen to our favorite love song or rock ballad, we create a mental association or emotional connection to what we are hearing. Sometimes we recall the first time we heard a particular song and then recall our feelings at the time. We wax nostalgic or respond negatively if the association was an unpleasant one. For this reason, advertising agencies and production houses use original music. This is a safe and often less costly option as the royalties are not as expensive as tunes that are immediately recognized. The danger is that some known melodies may not contribute to this new message. When done successfully, music we recognize in a commercial, for example, does exactly that: connects us on an emotional level. The music may relate to the product in a unique, funny, or interesting way. Product jingles reign supreme when it comes to this concept. Like slogans, musical jingles have the highest retention with the audience over just about any other device. "Oh I wish I were an Oscar Meyer wiener...". I bet you heard the tune in your head when you read the last sentence...I rest my case.

Why this is important to the voice actor is multifaceted. First, knowing the jingle or choice of music is useful for interpretation. Second, if you are voicing a product that has an established, recognizable jingle or bed, then you can match the delivery style and energy to these signature elements. It may seem like common sense, but all too often the actor loses out because they ignore the production values that might already be established. Third, you may be asked to sing the jingle. No kidding! Just look at how many commercials use actors singing the product or service. Many times the actor you are seeing is not the voice you are hearing. If you are not a singer, that's OK. It is not a requirement for voice work, but I have found that having a musical background can influence or reinforce creative choices the voice actor makes.

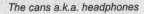
The cans a.k.a. headphones

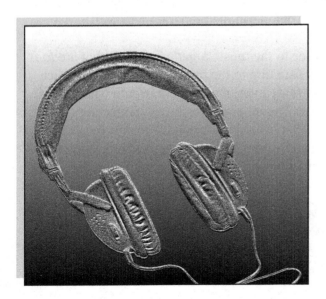

Music has an important place within the voice-over world. It can be a major contributor to the overall effectiveness of the spot and can influence the image that the advertising agency has worked so hard to develop. The talent's job is to integrate this ingredient so that whatever is being created becomes a cohesive, well-crafted, unified statement.

Adding a music bed or underscore to your work usually happens in post-production (after the voice is recorded). There are times when knowing the music can have an immediate impact on your performance. If there is music in the work you are doing, see if it is possible to listen to a sample. One exercise I do in class is to play music and have the actor imagine a spot it would work for. This is an excellent way of finding creative avenues for interpretation. Listening to the choices almost instantly suggests the mood, energy and persona. It's also quite an important consideration when we explore what works best when assembling an effective voice-over demo. In animation or narration, music, sound effects and even other characters are added post-production.

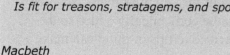

Exercise:

Play any instrumental cut from different recordings you may own. They can be in any genre such as, jazz, classical, rock, or pop. Select several commercials or promos from any of our exercises and see what sounds most effective with the choices you make. Make notations on the best selections for each read. How do your choices compare to what you have been hearing on TV or radio?

"The man that hath no music in himself,

Nor is not mov'd with concord of sweet sounds,

Is fit for treasons, stratagems, and spoils."

Macbeth

Inside the Fish Bowl

When looking at the importance of production in voice-over work, perhaps the most important person is that of the Sound Engineer. They are the technical artisans responsible for the audio, namely the projects' recording and editing. Their value cannot be overstated when it comes to supporting the performer in any recording session. It is also important to understand that long after your session is over, the engineer is still working to add the various elements (music, sound effects, ambient noise, equalization, tonal adjustments, special effects, etc.) to create the best possible result. One task that demands rigorous attention is that of editing. Cataloguing the best vocal *takes* and then putting them together by cutting, trimming and rendering what you have done is often tedious. It is useful to understand how you can assist in making the sound engineer's job as easy as possible.

I am not a sound engineer, but I have learned about some of the technical aspects while working as an administrator of broadcast training schools for twelve years. Here is what might help the voice actor present themselves in a positive light within the *fish bowl* (behind the glass in a sound studio). First, the more you are able to record, without stopping, the better. Extended recordings (book reads for example) will become a technical nightmare for the sound engineer if they must edit every other sentence. The longer the individual "take", the better it is for everyone. Next, proper breathing means NOT having excessive or audible inhaling or exhaling affectations. Proper, natural breathing is often left in recordings for a natural effect. If you wheeze or your inhalation is too noticeable, it can become a problem in post-production. With today's digital recording technology some issues can be fixed yet it is the performer that *does not present them* who gives the best professional impression.

Next, when you are directed in a session, it is often requested that you repeat a tag line or portion of the copy several different times and in different ways. This direction is normal. You must be able to insert a beat or pause between each read and change your inflection as many times as you can. In this way, the best delivery can be conveniently added to the final version. Keeping these simple, yet effective tips in mind can make a significant impression on the sound technician, not to mention your confidence.

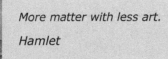

More matter with less art.

Hamlet

Directors Directing Directions Directly

I firmly believe that voice actors MUST have a trustworthy coach or teacher to help with choices in classes and in practice sessions. Yet, VO directors in recording sessions can be thought of in a variety of ways. By that, I mean there are times when you might not know the methodology of your director until you are both ready to record. Other times, directors are quite inspirational and know the precise vocabulary that is needed to get the desired performance out of you. In my experience, it is just like working on a film or stage project. The director can be challenged by the needs or issues of the performer. Conversely, the performer may have a difficult time understanding what the director is trying to communicate. In both cases, this can be a frustrating and uncreative situation. If there are any lessons to learn about your director or directors in general, it is this: you are responsible to do the best you can no matter what. It is also critical that you comprehend and execute requests made by the director. After all, you were booked for a reason. You won the job. It may simply become a matter of patience and tolerance when you are in session. There are directors that cannot easily express what they want. Do your best to understand, listen, nod, then *process* the notes. Additionally, you might see a look of confusion on his/her face when recording. This can become a growing frustration. Here are a few principles that might help if you find yourself in similar situations:

- ***Remember that the director is NOT your teacher:*** This might surprise some actors as it is the director that can be the "final" say about your work. They are not there to instruct you, however. What I find works better for me is to approach the director as a collaborator, someone who wants to participate in the best work you can do. If you automatically switch on the, "authority" protocol, you will ultimately surrender some creative influence. Rather, a peer to peer relationship can ultimately create better, more satisfying results. It is important to note that the director should be expecting this dynamic, most are. Yet, there are still some personality types who prefer to demonstrate their directorial control over the talent. Do your best to remain sensitive to this, and also, stay confident about your contribution to the project.

- ***Maintain your perspective:*** Having a moment to really analyze the situation will help you gain better understanding of what is happening. It is not brain surgery. It is not life threatening. It IS a moment in time when you have an opportunity to express your talent, creative abilities, AND get paid for it!

- ***Display confidence without being cocky:*** I use a saying all the time to help me when I feel insecure. It's "Act as if...". Behave *as if* I am confident and secure. If I am an actor, then I can take on the role of a secure actor. It's that simple. I don't mean letting my ego take over my basic sensibilities and be less than pleasant, professional and decent. That would be a serious mistake. Being just an ego with feet is rarely remembered except for the wrong reasons. Not good.

- ***Breathe:*** Remember that once you get the booking and have been hired, there is no valid reason to let your nerves participate in your session. Back to square breathing my friend! Being in control is the key to feeling creative. Really. Allowing your talent to express itself in a safe, positive, atmosphere is not always easy, but by applying ways to deflect the negative influences of other people and their nervousness is a matter of remembering to breathe. (Like after that last sentence!)

Not to get all touchy-feely here, but I have found it useful to put myself in the place of the director when communication seems rocky. Often, I find that even though I am not a psychologist, I can often *diagnose* some basic issues and feel compassionate rather than defensive. It helps to not remain focused strictly on myself and my own feelings but on the situation as it is presented. I can tell you that it has served me quite well many times over. Finally, I embrace the joy of performance and the fun that often takes place in recording sessions. I take the work quite seriously but, over time, I have learned and continue to learn, that I not to take myself too seriously. This is a much better way of embracing my professional journey. I try to not be a reactor to situations and circumstances that I have no control over.

Perhaps you might benefit from trying some of these suggestions. They could prove useful to your well-being not to mention your technique.

Producers Producing Productions Productively

The role of the producer in voice-over work varies greatly from project to project. If, for example, you are voicing narration for a documentary film, the producer will oversee the entire project. Creative decisions may or may not involve the producer. Sometimes those decisions are left to the director. The producer working at a production house that specializes in commercial work will, most likely, be the only decision- maker (along with a casting director) for the entire project. Their job is complex and frequently stressful. Producers are often the *managers* of the financial aspects or budgets of a given project. The success or failure of a finished product rests solely on the producer's shoulders. You can imagine, therefore, how interaction with the talent on the set or in the studio is somewhat limited. I have found it best not to engage a producer during a booking. It's reminiscent of the parental advice" don't speak until spoken to". I don't mean to sound harsh or cold here, it really is a matter of, once again, being sensitive to the environment in which you are working.

There is a component to being a producer that I would like to address. It is when the producer feels compelled to add creative feedback (which is usually reserved for the director). There are even times when the producer will privately or even publicly offer critiques and/or suggestions as to how to perform *better*. This can be quite a dilemma for the voice actor. What would you do if the director gave you a specific note on what to do and then the producer asks for a completely contrary or different interpretation? Well, I can share with you what I have done in the past when this happens. I nod, smile, thank whoever for the "great" suggestion and then do my best to try *both* out separately. Understand that you are not a punching bag for everyone that has an idea. You are, however, expected to have the skill level to make spontaneous adjustments when asked for...to the best of your ability!

More Creative Team Players Playing

Other production players you may need to be aware of in an audition or a recording session include casting directors, writers, and advertising agency executives. Here is a brief overview of these creative folks behind the scenes:

• *The writer:* He/she has either been independently hired or work for the advertising agency to create the copy for you to perform. Good copy writers have an instinctive knack for targeting the right tone and energy in their writing for a successful project. There are times when the writer is on hand for last minute changes that are asked for. On another note, be very careful when you are discussing the material. Creative "types" are sensitive folks who might not take too kindly to a snide remark or negative aside. They have their job to do just as you have yours.

- *The casting director:* Is hired by the producer to help qualify the talent for the project. Many times, there are specific criteria that are used to fulfill the requirements needed for a commercial. The casting director schedules appointments with the talent agents and may often "pre-screen" talent making sure everyone who eventually auditions for the final decision makers are excellent choices, based on the vision of the creative team. Casting directors can be independent, meaning they work on a variety of different projects while some casting directors are exclusive to the ad agency or production house. Even though they are hired by the producers, they want the talent to succeed. After all, it makes their job much easier if you match what is being asked for.

- *Advertising agency executives:* Are involved in the entire process of commercial production. From initial concept to the final edits of the spots, the advertising agency executive is completely responsible for the success or failure of an ad campaign. They can also function in a producer capacity, hiring the creative team or they are solely invested in the entire process. They are hired by the company needing the advertising and answer to the needs of that company. As you can imagine, there is a lot of stress and pressure placed upon these folks.

So, as you can see, your contribution to the overall success of any given promotion, commercial, production or announcement is valued and yet, considered *one* piece of the puzzle. Being a professional team player when working with any or all of these talented, creative individuals can offer you a rewarding, successful journey and allow your best work to shine.

Jeff's notebook

I can always find something positive about any given project that I am working on. It is important to be a supportive influence during a recording session, for example, and not just a temporary hire known as "the talent". Also, I think it is important to share my thoughts with those that might appreciate the support. Being truthfully nice is better than just saying something nice though.

Tools of the Trade

You've worked on your performance techniques, understood and dissected the copy, and comprehended the dynamics of production. With all this knowledge you might think you are ready to go. Go where? If you would like to get hired doing voice-overs, then there are specific materials that are needed. First, you'll need an industry-acceptable *package* that will bypass amateur status and launch your career. That is what this next section is all about. First, we will look at the demo. This is the recorded sampling of your voice work assembled in a creative, comprehensive and impressive way. We will look at a brief history of demonstration recordings and understand how today's digital technology can ease your own demo effort. We will also reveal the absolute best way to cast yourself perfectly for what goes on the demo. Next, we will look at another important tool, marketing your talent to the right people. Those who are looking for you to voice their product or service. Also, what is an agent and what can they do for you? How do you advertise yourself? Finally, we will examine the industry itself; the business dynamics and how it is structured. This will assist in your ability to find constructive ways to promote your talent to it's fullest advantage.

What are your expectations for yourself and this next step? Before we get to the nuts and bolts, take a moment and think about the goals you have set up for yourself. Do you use a time frame? Perhaps you prefer to set up task oriented goals. This examination can be an important and useful exercise. It provides an opportunity to realistically address the best course of action for what you are seeking. Further, it can help address some of the issues when things go wrong. From my experience, I have learned to accept the outcome, no matter what. From finding the right agent to making the best demo to getting the job, having realistic expectations is healthy. I must admit, it took quite a bit of trial and error before I could embrace the concept of obtainable goals. My insecurities and low self esteem took me down various negative, self defeating paths. I would not wish that journey on anyone, yet, I have no regrets. Each and every negative situation eventually revealed a larger positive purpose. My love of performing kept me anchored to the focused, *realistic* goals I set for myself. Perhaps this advice is useful to you as well. Remember that as you travel forward with your plan, you must keep your expectations reasonable. That is to say, it never hurts to dream big, but do it with your eyes open.

Let's look at how the demo got its start.

Demo Retrospective

The origins of demonstration recordings for voice work are not completely known. Logic dictates that when commercial radio was coming into its "Golden Age" (from 1925 to 1950), the announcer was vital to the medium. Almost exclusively male, the deep bass voice accomplished several important functions. First, because the quality of the signal was often poor, the bass voice was easier to understand. The pitch worked well for the technology. Next, the strong male voice was more readily accepted as an authority for news and advertisements. Hearing the virtues of any given product or service by a dominant male voice was thought to instill a commanding *call to action*. The advent of radio drama, comedy, and variety entertainment introduced the female voice to the industry. Female characters in these drama or comedy productions offered qualities that the listener could identify with. Talent that was used in the early days of radio usually came from the Broadway stage. Actors whose trained voices could project and enunciate clearly in the theater became indispensable to this newly created technology. Performances were live, meaning that whatever you were listening to was being performed in *real time* or it was aired via recordings on phonograph records.

It wasn't until the advent of magnetic recording tape that voice talent was given the opportunity to assemble their work into a sample "reel" known as demonstration recording (or demo reel). For those who were working "on air" the talent could submit their shows and commercials to other stations or networks for hiring consideration. If a performer was just entering the profession or going from a small market radio station to a larger one, the demo became the calling card. Whether it was for announcing, hosting, singing, or news broadcasting, what you sounded like was essential to the consideration you were given. Sound reels were sent, hand delivered, or "pitched" by the talent themselves or by a new type of show business talent representative, known as the agent. The reels were often 7 or 14 inches in diameter and anywhere from 15-45 minutes long, depending on the specific request made by the job seeker. As time and technology added demands on the industry, the demo became more specific to the hiring opportunities available. 7 inch reels of anywhere between 10 to 20 minutes in length became the norm. Actors voiced commercials, announcers introduced shows (later disk jockeys came into the picture) and news broadcasters gave their best performance "takes" with their demo tape reels.

The next substantial change in voice-over technology was the advent of the cassette tape. This small version of larger, bulky reel to reel recorder technology meant that everyone could now record themselves and promote their work much more effectively. Advertising agencies now collected voice samples for their clients. Actors and broadcasters had a cheap method of "sampling" their skills to anyone who was interested. The length of the recordings changed dramatically as well. Usually five minutes of material was all that was needed to establish your skill and abilities. As talent evolved their unique style into their performances, the demo was used to capture it. Production, editing and "skimming" (a method of capturing the voice while on the air) contributed to the success of the voice-over industry. The methods of marketing and promoting voice talent continued to advance as technology evolved in this *digital age*.

The CD became the standard media of choice for voice-overs when the personal computer became commonplace. Now, very high quality recordings ruled the day. Digital editing, packaging, producing and promoting became essential to the success of talent looking for work. Previous samples of 2 to 4 minutes was now reduced to one to two minutes. It seems safe to say that as technology grew, the attention span of the listener shortened considerably. Casting directors, advertising agencies, agents, managers, station owners and cable channels only needed a few seconds to discern whether or not you were given an Audition, booking or meeting.

With the tremendous growth of the internet, the voice talent industry has found ways to exploit this phenomenon to its advantage. Websites dedicated to voice talent libraries, individual promotion of talent via their own website and talent agencies' promotion via the web is now thought of as the norm. Now it is even possible to voice anything from your own home studio and send it anywhere in the world.

What the future holds is anyone's guess. Human performers will still be needed for communicating the uniqueness that can only be found in the individual voice. Using the latest methods for assembling your demo tape is the best way to ensure promotional success and marketing effectiveness now and in the future.

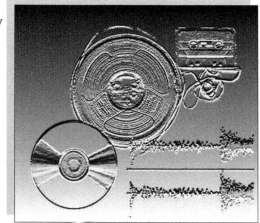

Media evolution portrait: *top left to bottom right, reel of magnetic tape, cassette tape, compact disk, digital sound signal.*

Workshop Workout

Voice-over Self Evaluation

Complete this page to the best of your ability. Do not omit anything. After you have completed this page, you will use many of the answers for choosing your demonstration compilation material, also known as the demo.

Three television/radio commercials that I could have been hired for voice acting are:
1._____ 2._____
3._____

My top three favorite magazines that I read or have read recently are:
1._____ 2._____
3._____

Characters or personalities that I most resemble:
1._____ 2._____
3._____

All adjectives that can describe my NORMAL speaking voice:

☐ Masculine	☐ Sexy	☐ Sad	☐ Quirky
☐ Feminine	☐ Gruff	☐ Energetic	☐ Childish
☐ High Pitched	☐ Smooth	☐ Fast	☐ Elderly
☐ Low Pitched	☐ Soft	☐ Slow	☐ Youthful
☐ Sweet	☐ Hard	☐ Weak	☐ _____
☐ Smokey	☐ Funny	☐ Loud	☐ _____

My age range is: _____

Accents that I can perform with confidence: _____ _____
_____ _____ _____

Regionalisms that I can perform with confidence: _____ _____
_____ _____ _____

I read out loud every day: Yes ☐   No ☐
My dream voice-over job would be:

_____
_____.

Commercial Demo Voice Choice

Some of the items on the last exercise seem obvious when deciding what to include on a demo of your best work. Some may seem superfluous. Self knowledge can be vital when casting your material or script choices. After you have filled it out, let's discuss the demo from two points of view: its basic purpose and its intended purpose.

The basic purpose for a demo is to offer a sample of your vocal performance skills. A variety of material with which you skillfully represent yourself is what is required. Only commercials and narrations you believe match your voice should be considered. Recall the last workout question that asked for commercial examples you could identify with. This is the first step in your selection process. Next, by writing down the magazines you read regularly, you narrowed your *demographic* to your own age, gender and ethnicity. Now, look through those magazines and you will find a virtual treasure trove of written copy that works for your demo recording. The copy might need some editing, but make no mistake, what is being advertised is a perfect roadmap of what you need to use. Without over-evaluating the choices, write or, better yet, cut out the ads that appeal to you the most. Ask yourself why they appeal to you. It may be the humor, content, character or other unique characteristic. This exercise is great fun and can inspire you to take risks that you might not otherwise take.

Now let's approach the demo using its intended purpose for perspective. If you are an accomplished voice-over artist, there is a good chance that your best work is "cut" into your demo. You probably have several brief samples providing various moods and interpretations that show you off. As a newcomer, you need to have a polished demo even though you may not have professional experience yet. The big secret is...Shhh...your demo just needs to *sound* like you are an accomplished voice-over artist commercials, promo's and narrations that represent you as having done the work already. By adding production, judicious editing, and strong performances in a crisp and dynamic *sounding* demo, you will have made the professional impression you seek. That is why using material showing your strongest vocal assets and casting yourself well is so important. The work page on page 67 is one method of choosing commercial copy that suits you. You can create scripts in every VO category using these techniques. Here are some helpful steps:

"My words fly up, my thoughts remain below: Words without thoughts never to heaven go."- Hamlet

- ***Pick material that matches how you would be cast:*** "Where do I look for copy?" is a question that I get asked frequently. On the work page found on page 64, you listed three top magazines that you read. Now just open any one of these and check out the advertisements. The best copy is right in front of you! The magazine ads and some articles are chock full of superbly written copy. You may have to tweak it so that it scans for brevity. This is very easy, especially now that you have the foundation of good copywriting techniques. What you should look for are the very best first or last lines of copy: brief "liners" that are one or two sentences in length. Believe it or not, sometimes it can be just an ad's tag line. "Spice it up with Zaterans!" is an example. By using magazines you read, you are actually picking the spots that are meant for your demographic or the commercials that you would actually get hired to voice. As you research your choices it is important to filter down the best candidates. Let the mood of each printed advertisement assist you with the particular style you wish to convey. For example, if you see a couple in an embrace on the beach, it would be a good guess to envision a sensual sounding VO. Now, compare the other choices you like and ask yourself "What am I showing with this copy that I have not shown in others?" In other words, variety AND versatility in the copy are critical to your casting decisions. Do not limit yourself to just conservative easy choices. Fun, serious, interesting copy should be considered. See the next page for an example of this type of extrapolation!

- ***Rehearse each one separately:*** Use as much of the advertisement or article as you need to give yourself a clear intention of who you are playing. Remember that your demo will only be a very brief *taste* of the entire commercial or narration. By rehearsing longer sections and then cutting in (editing) the desired section later, you will have set the mood, pace and character for each of your reads. Be very careful that you do not practice or rehearse your choices back to back. This is not a good idea as it is next to impossible to shift from one persona and mood to another. Better to work each one using all the performance techniques you have learned before moving on to the next one. Keep a mental separation of your performances during this entire process until each has been thoroughly explored for its usefulness to your demo's concept.

- ***Choose the placement order of the demo:*** The order of the demo is based on the practical and creative choices you make. Which clip should the listener hear first? Next? This decision has several components to it that need to be considered. Generally speaking, the first cut on the demo would probably be a sampling of your most "bookable" work. By this, I mean a performance that shows off what you are especially well-suited for. Next, the best choice would be something upbeat, funny. Followed by a sincere/sad PSA (public service announcement).

Continued on page 68

Workshop Workout

Creative Script Dehydration

Use any typical magazine advertisement (this is an example) and "re-write" for a voice-over. These mini copy selections are perfect for using on a demo tape. This is especially true if it is from a magazine that you might typically buy and read; why? Because it matches your demographic and therefore is copy you would get cast in!

Magazine advertisement

Edited Copy

Can scientists and beauty experts agree?

Milky Wonder

PROFESSIONAL

Works as well as a leading prescription for reducing the look of fine lines and wrinkles.

PROFESSIONAL Milky Wonder

Beauty experts and scientist agree that professional Milky Wonder is not just effective but is considered cutting edge technology for younger beautiful skin. Milky Wonder is the only beauty skin treatment proven and backed by science and skin experts.

Milky Wonder   ...Professional... Proven... Perfect

Scientists and beauty experts agree, Milky Wonder works as well as a leading prescription brand for reducing the look of wrinkles. Professional Milky Wonder is considered cutting edge technology.

Voice-over demo Copy

Reduce the look of wrinkles with science and experts behind it! Milky Wonder professional ...Professional and proven...perfect!

Jeff's Notebook

Note: Clean look and clinical layout make the mood feel professional, medical and direct...the delivery should reflect the visual presentation that is present. Also, notice the visual cues for style, humor, personality.

This is one avenue of pursuit when you are trying to determine the best order. Please note there is no hard and fast definitive order that works for everyone. Additionally, different categories will require separate script choices for each category. Commercials, narrations, promos, and book reads need to be presented as individual demos.

Keep in mind that you do not need to *become* several personalities in your characterizations. Just samples that you are confident portraying in a professional manor. There is no sense in playing the part of someone you cannot easily recreate in a studio environment or audition.

Another component that needs to be considered here is what I call *rational limitations*. If you have defined yourself as a spokesperson, a clear, naturally friendly-sounding person with authority, then you may elect to limit the number of choices to what you are comfortable with. The style of delivery, mood, and energy can and should be varied but that does not imply you should be different just for the sake of it. The best decisions can be made when you put yourself in the ear of the listener. What sustains interest? What dynamics are appealing for each choice? Have you picked the best examples of what *you* can do? What, if anything is missing? Remember that there is no cookie cutter approach here. As an actor, YOU are the decider of what you want to market and how. The demo is no different. I like to make sure that the order and placement a student chooses best exemplifies their personality in circumstances and situations. Everyone is challenged by trying to be objective about their copy choices. It is always a good idea to get feedback from a trusted, experienced person who will critique your selections and in what order to place them. If you select the material and order that is entertaining, creative and comprehensive in scope, then you have succeeded.

Something to think about...

*Every type of demo, whether it is a commercial, promo, narration or animation sample should not exceed 1:00 minute TOTAL. No one will listen to more than that when they are evaluating you. Really. Even though you may **love** everything you do, be judicious and creative with your editing. It is much more impressive for listeners to want to hear more rather than hearing too much.*

This above all: to thine own self be true.

Hamlet

Workshop Workout
Voice-over Demo Sampler

Irish character
Come to the new fresh scent of *Irish Spring*! The deodorant soap that lasts all day. Made for a man but the lass will like it too. *Irish Spring*

British Character
It's terribly sad to miss the nooks and crannies…Ta Da! *Thomas' English Muffins* to the rescue.

Southern Character
J & B Auto Parts. Complete domestic and foreign auto parts for your car or truck. For the professional or do-it-your-selfer!

Sexy
Yes…yes…yes…yes…yes…it's at times like this when *Herbal Essence shampoo* is better than… you know.

Italian or your choice
Prego Old World Style versus Ragu. You can see the difference. *Prego* is thick, full of vegetables and good taste. Ragu is thin because it has no vegetables. *Prego*…it's better!

Cheesy Agent
Hey Babe…love the demo…we'll have to do lunch sometime OK? Give me a ring. Ciao for now!

Promo personas
The Winter Olympics…now on DVD…share a moment with the world.

Coming up next, the 10 best embarrassing moments ever, right here on *E Entertainment Network*.

These are the movies on *A & E*…time well spent.

This is the world of *Public Television*…come join it with us.

It's easy to see why we still have questions. Watch *Haunting Places on The Travel Channel*.

Real Person
Hey Sprint users…you've never heard sound this clear…*AT&T True Voice*.

O.K. son, it's time you knew the truth about birds and bees...uh, they, they both...can fly...real fast.

Depression…it can affect you in ways you would never suspect…because depression can be a lot more than just the blues.

When I need a "get away from it all" moment…I just reach for my *Bit O' Honey*. Yum…delicious.

Think of the Rockies as a big block of ice. Now consider us a chip off the old block. *Coors Light,* Silver bullet smooth.

Hyper Real
Time is running out on the best-selling Disney video of all time. So hurry and buy *Snow White*…*the collectors edition,* while they last.

Workshop Workout

(Continued from previous page)

Who says you can't afford dental insurance? **Crest** is the dentist's choice!

Because even little people get big coughs and colds...**Robitussin Pediatric**.

Get ready to taste the future...New **Ice Draft from Budweiser**

Yes!...you don't have to say no to rich, creamy, smooth, **Jell-O Instant Pudding**!

Animated character
The best way to wrap sandwiches is finally out of the bag. **Reynolds Wrap**!

Never rub a tub the wrong way...**Soft Scrub**...the right way!

Once upon a time you needed Peter Pan to make dreams come true. Now all you need is a Magic Palace. **Walt Disney World**...once upon a time is here.

Yumm...Yum...Yum...New **Yum Yum's**...tastes so crunchy good, you'll need <u>me</u> to keep em safe!

Tough
Sometimes, you don't know when you're gonna die, you just end up that way...**Night Visions**...rated R.

Rough Trucks...**US Monster Hotrod wars**.

Duralast batteries...meant to last. The strength to keep on keepin' on.

Dreamy escape
Coffee so enchanting you'll fall in love. **General Foods International coffees**.

My lover has something no one else has...me. **Me**...new from the makers of Oil of Olay.

*Dual Character
Hey! Wanna buy my car? It runs like brand new. Hey, you on the corner...that bus'll never come. Wanna buy my car? (ad lib with funny additional shouts)
Tag: If you really want to sell your car...take an ad out in the **New York Times**.

Sofa for sale. It's a real good deal. Almost new. Sofa for sale. Free delivery to the highest bidder. Sofa for sale. (ad lib with funny additional shouts).
Tag: If you really want to sell your sofa...take an ad out in **The New York Times**.

Elf: ...And so the most important thing is to not be naughty but nice...and have a **Canon color printer**.
Interviewer: **A Canon color printer?** Why?
Elf...So that you can have a crisp, clear, colorful list...so that you can fax the big man!
Interviewer: Oh, I see...that make sense...I guess.
Elf: Don't guess...or else you're on the naughty list! ...Just kidding.

*Note: Dual Character means you are playing both. Record each one separately and overlap some of the dialog for an impressive result.

70

Workshop Workout

Commercial Voice-over Demo Sampler Checklist

List the best choices you have for placement in your commercial demo. Next, arrange the choices in numerical order with check boxes selected for definitions/options to consider. Remember that production variety and vocal versatility are the important factors to consider, while contrasting choices are equally important factors to consider. Your choices should reflect your abilities and casting potential. This is meant to be an example and may not work for every category of commercial demo!

🕐	Name of Spot:	#	Character/ Personality	Production Elements:

Bookable/Bankable ☐

Fun/Light ☐

Character ☐

Straight announce ☐

Driving/Fast ☐

Sincere/ Empathetic ☐

Fun/Light ☐

Unusual/ Off beat ☐

Animation ☐

Notes: _____

_____

_____

_____

🕐 _____

TOTAL TIME :<:60   Slate/Out take:_____

Animated Arguments

Animation demos have very specific qualifications and unwritten rules that can make the selection of the right material quite important. Usually the better examples include characters **you** have created. One method is to write a scene that includes all your character voices. These must be recorded as individual lines of conversation and edited together post-production. Do not try to switch back and forth from one character to another when recording. It is virtually impossible to make this successful. The reason is simple; when we hear your breath and when you try to physically sound different, it is a dead giveaway. This can sound completely amateurish. Another method is to combine a "medley" of individual characters in rapid fire succession without regard to continuity. They can be scripted (you could record a pre-existing show or production and transcribe it, for example) or from copy you write. Scripts that capture similarities to actual spots or shows works well. This is a strong choice when going from a video game to, let's say, a cartoon to an inanimate talking product. Be careful to choose this method only if you can show clear delineation in your portrayal from one character to another. If you sound the same it simply won't work. Finally, if you are uncomfortable with several voices, one or two characters with longer scripting is the way to go. The challenge with longer scripts is Self-evident. You must sustain our interest throughout the entire read. The material and the performances need to be extremely captivating and dynamic.

Production components are also equally important. Remember that your demo should have all the qualities of being aired already. Sound effects and appropriate background music should work together with your script. In addition to your production elements, it is assumed that you are NOT using digital techniques to embellish your voice. Manipulation in post-production like speeding the pace, pitch and other effects (on your voice) will almost automatically discount you for any consideration. Some bass enhancement or EQ (equalization refers changing the sound frequencies for various sound dynamics) can be used, albeit sparingly. Rather than feeling constrained by what seems like rather limited choices, researching, writing and creative presentation can be quite fun...not to mention rewarding. You can find several music beds and sound effects on the web for free. By incorporating excellent production effects with your performance and thereby creating an interesting, fun, adventurous and surprising demo of which you can be proud is the answer. Taking time with every aspect is the best way to go about it.

72

Audiobook and Narration: Bound and Gagged

Choosing the material that should go on a narration demo or audio-book has the same challenges that you might have for a commercial demo. It should be noted that this type of demo needs to be separate from a commercial demo, just as an animation reel needs to be presented separately from any other demo. (An exception would be having an animation voice or two toward the end or interspersed into your commercial reel). What you choose must accomplish several things for effective narration.

- ***Your choices must be a good match to your vocal abilities:*** The best way to learn what works is to listen to several book and narration performances and match the type of material to your own voice qualities.

- ***Pick a section of material that is interesting:*** Remember that you must be able to sustain the listener's interest. Why choose something that is tedious or boring?

- ***Have three or four different selections with varying degrees of performance styles:*** A children's story could be followed by a technical manual segment then followed by a first person narrative.

Match your interest, vocal quality and performance techniques to choices that fit *you*. If, for example, you are able to "suggest" several characters in a story, then you would be well advised to pick a story that does exactly that. Not that you should become different people by changing your voice, but present a variation on the narrator's persona when another character is speaking. You can accomplish this with vocal pitch, pace, energy level and musicality within your vocal range. Understand the differences in narration demos by listening to examples of them. Creating atmosphere and interest within the narration is vital to a good performance. Warm, authoritative presentation skills are a must for this kind of work. Also, because of the physical demands this work requires, you must be able to read out loud for long continuous periods of time. Presenting yourself as a narrator implies that you can meet this challenge. Ironically, your demo needs to have just three or four strong selections amounting to no more than :60 seconds total time. The listener must be able to follow the story without the voice sounding monotonous or tedious. Make sure that you have rehearsed the material completely. Taking the time to test different intonation, delivery and energy styles is time well spent. Sounding confident and in complete control of the material will only come with practice and patience. This can be a rewarding exercise not only for your demo but for keeping the audition and performance "muscles" in shape.

Workshop Workout

Audiobook Script Sampler

Test yourself and record several (if not all) of the following samples. Now, play them back with specific notes on the choices you made. Do your choices meet the necessary presentation criteria?

• "Winston had disliked her from the very first moment of seeing her. He knew the reason. It was because of the atmosphere of hockey fields and cold baths and community hikes and general clean mindedness which she managed to carry about her. He disliked nearly all women, and especially the young and pretty ones, who were the most bigoted adherents of the party, the swallowers of slogans, the amateur spies and nosers out of unorthodoxy."
  George Orwell, *1984*, Book 1

• "Nearly all children nowadays were horrible. What was worst of all was that by means of such organizations as the Spies they were systematically turned into ungovernable little savages, and yet this produced in them no tendency whatever to rebel against the discipline of the Party. On the contrary, they adored the Party and everything connected with it... All their ferocity was turned outwards, against the enemies of the State, against foreigners, traitors, saboteurs, thought criminals. It was almost normal for people over thirty to be frightened of their own children." George Orwell, *1984*, Book 1

• "Mr. Justice Wargrave thought to himself: 'Armstrong? Remember him in the witness box. Very correct and cautious. All doctors are damned fools. Harley Street ones are the worst of the lot.' And his mind dwelt malevolently on a recent interview he had had with a suave personage in that very street." Agatha Christie, *And Then There Were None*

• "It had become usual to give Napoleon the credit for every successful achievement and every stroke of good fortune. You would often hear one hen remark to another, 'Under the guidance of our Leader, Comrade Napoleon, I have laid five eggs in six days'; or two cows, enjoying a drink at the pool, would exclaim, 'Thanks to the leadership of Comrade Napoleon, how excellent this water tastes!'" George Orwell, *Animal Farm*

• "Alpha children wear grey. They work much harder than we do, because they're so frightfully clever. I'm awfully glad I'm a Beta, because I don't work so hard. And then we are much better than the Gammas and Deltas. Gammas are stupid. They all wear green, and Delta children wear khaki. Oh no, I don't want to play with Delta children. And Epsilons are still worse. They're too stupid to be able to read or write. Besides they wear black, which is such a beastly color. I'm so glad I'm a Beta." Aldous Huxley, *Brave New World*

• "Cannery Row in Monterey in California is a poem, a stink, a grating noise, a quality of light, a tone, a habit, a nostalgia, a dream. Cannery Row is the gathered and scattered, tin and iron and rust and splintered wood, chipped pavement and weedy lots and junk heaps, sardine canneries of corrugated iron, honky tonks, restaurants and whore houses, and little crowded groceries, and laboratories and flophouses." John Steinbeck, *Cannery Row*

Workshop Workout

Documentary Narration Script Sampler

- AMERICAN GOTHIC, *The Learning Channel*

In 1930 an Iowa artist named Grant Wood asked his sister and his dentist to pose for a painting, a tribute to the tough rural stock of America. He dressed his sister in a simple frock, a white collar held close around her neck by a brooch. The dentist he outfitted in overalls, a band collar shirt, buttoned tight around the throat, a dark business jacket. He posed the couple, board stiff in front of a plain house. The man, transformed by art into a Midwestern farmer, grips a pitchfork and stares straight ahead. The woman looks away. The resulting painting, called American Gothic, became one of the most enduring images of the decade, an icon of the spirit that survived the hard times of the Depression.

- CHESTER, CT, *The Travel Channel*

Nestled in the rolling hills of the Connecticut River Valley, Chester is a lovely New England village. The charming winding roads, interesting shops, and friendly people greet the visitor and resident alike. Originally known as Pattaquonk Quarter, Chester was settled in 1692. Many mills sprang up as settlers established permanent homes and Chester became the Fourth Parish of Saybrook. By 1836, it became an independent town. Travel in the early days was by river, so the ship-building industry was an important part of the town's beginnings. Several modern marinas now dot the riverfront, as well as two yacht clubs.

- DEER, *Animal Planet*

The deer approaches the opening, unaware of the cougar's presence. Slowly and quietly, Shuka creeps toward his prey. Hearing a twig crack, the deer turns and faces impending danger. There is no time to run before the six-foot-long, 200 pound make cougar pounces on its back and bites its neck. The deer, a favorite food of the cougar has met its match. He has fallen victim to the balance of nature.

- GALAPAGOS ISLANDS, *National Geographic Channel*

Perhaps the most amazing thing about the animals of the Galapagos, is not how they look, but that they seem to know no fear of humans. Most of the Galapagos Islands have no permanent human settlements. Still, people have stopped to visit throughout history. But we remain enough of a rarity here that instead of running away, most animals move in for a closer look.

Jeff's notebook

When you have found great scripts in the right category for yourself, rehearsed them diligently and put them in a sequential order that is both compelling and dynamic, it feels great! It is time to record your choices and produce the demo for a finished product.

Master Recording

Now comes the most challenging aspect of demo preparation: the recording. It seems that everyone has an opinion on how to do this. I will mention a handful of suggestions to help you with this decision. Keep in mind that you may have your own methods or preferences. Remember that the goal is to have clips of various material that contain the proper performance and production criteria of being produced already. Use the recording method that best fits this profile for you.

• *With a relatively minimal financial investment, you could purchase the necessary tools for a home studio:* If you already own a computer or laptop, then a good condenser mic, headset and reliable recording/ production software is all you might need. The physical area in which you record must be free from ANY excess noise including hard surfaces where the sound might echo back to the microphone. I know actors who set up their mini studio in a closet. The sound-deadening properties of hanging clothing work well. Also, it is assumed that you have a strong working knowledge of the recording software and can edit music beds, sound effects and other elements onto a hard drive and then burn a CD. Taking a class, asking a friend and teaching yourself are all viable options. Remember not to skimp on the microphone. This is probably the most important purchase you will make. An excellent quality mic really does make a difference. Finally, if you plan on going into the VO business, then this should be considered as part of your startup costs. Many times auditions and even bookings can be done at home and sent via the internet. You will be glad you made the right choice of quality tools.

• *You might have a friend or could make a friend who can record the work for you using their equipment and expertise in production:* Perhaps a local college or high school would assist you in their facility. Some sound design students could use the experience for their portfolio. Local radio stations have may production facilities and personnel who would appreciate the attention and/or nominal payment. There are many creative ways of getting your work recorded and edited.

• *Hire a professional studio that includes a capable production technician:* This is the most expensive option. On the positive side, the quality and convenience of giving the task to someone else is clearly obvious. There are downsides, such as unscrupulous studio businesses whose only interest is in taking your money. They often use a cookie cutter approach to demos and provide little room for creative input. Therefore, it is up to you to research as many studios as you can to decide what is comfortable for you.

(Continued on page 78)

Workshop Workout

Common computer digital sound editor/recorder

Although slightly different graphic user interface (GUI), they all have similar functions.

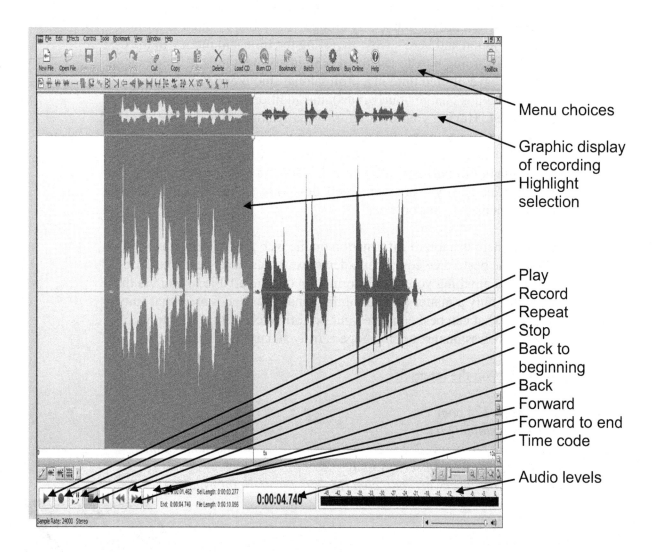

Menu choices

Graphic display
of recording

Highlight
selection

Play
Record
Repeat
Stop
Back to
beginning
Back
Forward
Forward to end
Time code

Audio levels

Something to think about...

Visually, the screen is set up like a tape recorder. A visual representation or graphic is displayed so that you can make adjustments to adjust the tracks you "lay down". Depending on the software, there are some variations on this user interface but most are quite easy to identify and can be learned quickly.

(continued from page 76)
This could take considerable time and resources. Also, be leery of internet businesses that promise professional services. Some companies or businesses will take your raw material and produce a finished product, but I have yet to hear one of these demos get results with bookings, agents or auditions. Buyer beware.

Whatever the method of recording you choose, keep the objective in mind. A professional sounding demo starts with a professional sounding voice. The production component is important but it should only be there to support you, not the other way around. I personally like the do-it-yourself option and here's why: investing the time and money in the best tools and learning how to use them is an investment in *you*. Think about it. If you have limited time in a professional studio and the clock is ticking (studios charge hourly rates), the additional pressure can be debilitating. Having your own setup virtually eliminates this pressure and assures you of having perfect sessions. Learning the production software can be fun and useful. Free software programs like ***Audacity*** (***www.audacity.com***) take little time to learn and can achieve professional results. Clearly, if you are completely devoid of technical ability, then the other options are your best bet.

Finally, there is a ton of information on the web for building your own studio, the best voice equipment, demo examples, copy resources, etc. Just about anything you need information on is available to you via the web. It is only a matter of determining what your needs are, what suits you and what can best enhance your performance ability. Giving your work a professional sounding edge is truly satisfying and rewarding.

Resources on the internet:

www.voice123.com
www.voicetalent.com
www.ehow.com/how_2133523_build-voice-over-studio-home.html
www.edgestudio.com/scripts.htm
www.thevoiceoverworkshop.com (My site for more information)

Jeff's notebook

I listen to other voice-over demos via the internet when I can. It's a great way to evaluate what is going on "out there" and will often inspire me to add something to my own work. I hate to say it, but there are also a lot of poor examples floating around in the internet universe. I believe you can learn from these demos as well. After all, knowing what doesn't work can be just as useful as knowing what does.

The Assembly Line

OK. You have recorded your liners and promos, edited spots and added your production music, sound effects and special effects. It is now time to use your workout checklist and assemble the various bits of sound into your final product. Make sure the music beds are not too prominent. Too many times the production of a commercial overshadows the performance. The performance needs the spotlight with the other elements acting as supporting features. There are some common errors that happen during this final stage of demo creation. Here are a few:

• **Levels vary too much:** When putting the demo together, make sure the volume levels are consistent with the rest of the recordings. There should be no reason for the listener to have to adjust the volume when listening. Equalizing the level of the recording is relatively easy, even in post-production.

• **Music is too prominent:** Again, this refers not only to the choice of music (recognizable tunes or music with lyrics, known artists etc.) which tend to draw attention away from the voice, but over-modulation detracts from the performance as well.

• **Spots sound the same**: Remember that as each *read* has its own performance personality, so too does the production criteria. The best method of determining what works best is to treat each choice as a completely separate entity. In other words, no two scripts should have similar features to the other. Changing the equalization to produce a television spot followed by a slight change to give an AM radio effect, etc. is suggestive of a realistic variety of "on air" samples. Additionally, remember also that the music and mood needs to demonstrate variety with every cut (edit).

• **Demo is not edited correctly:** This mistake is made during the final edit of the demo. There is an assumption that continuity within the individual spot is needed. In this case, we choose to let the music reach a natural conclusion before cutting in the next commercial. Sometimes we think it is important to add a beat of silence between reads to show separation between each one. Both of these choices can be deadly. Do not give the listener a chance to breathe or mentally pause from your demo. Edits should be very tight. Edits usually work well when they occur immediately after the name of the product or concluding thought.

"A mellifluous voice..."

Twelfth Night

Professionally Speaking

Now what? This is often the all too familiar question that seems to happen with voice talent. You've spent time researching your demographic, selecting the right script, recorded the voice track and added the production to create a first rate demo. Wonderful! The question still remains, "Now what?" How do you promote, market and sell your abilities so that you can actually get paid for your effort? That is what this chapter is about: realistic steps to move your new found skill into the professional arena. Clearly, each of you will have a unique journey with this step. Some of you may be in a location like New York or LA in which the opportunities are greater than, let's say, Cleveland. Others may decide to focus on more specific interests such as telephone voice prompts and voice-mail jobs. Still others may want to go into business for themselves. No matter which area that interests you, there are useful approaches and practical tips that can help.

Like any good business plan, it is vital for you to have a specific set of goals:

- What are your interests with voice work?
- What do you hope to accomplish?
- What would be a dream gig?
- What is a realistic strategy for giving your career a boost?

The more detailed and specific your answers, the better your plan. To simply mail out your demo to anyone you think may help, although not a bad idea, rarely produces results. A purposeful, professional and realistic approach is always a better choice. The next part of your plan is to *write down the answers to the questions at the beginning of this paragraph.* Again, be specific. You may decide to limit your steps to smaller, more easily obtainable goals. You may discover that there is a lot to learn about the industry first. In each of these cases, do not stress over this important list exercise. Remember that you have complete and total control over the decisions you make. This is not a burden, but rather a systematic series of decisions based on your drive, motivation, time frame and circumstances.

With a well constructed performance demo, marketing your talent can take on many options. One of the first steps to consider is to make several copies of the CD. A professional presentation is important. A sharp, attractive label with your contact phone number, perhaps your picture and location is essential. Just writing your name with a *sharpie* on a bare CD is destined for the trash heap. You do not need to spend a lot of money on professionally printed CD's. A clean, easily readable label is fine. If you are planning on going into business for yourself, then you should consider a company logo or other imaging statements that identify your businesses mission and talent presence. The CD is just one part of the package you will need to include in any mailing or marketing. The next item that usually accompanies the CD is the resume. A voice performer's resume is different than the typical business resume used in the corporate world. It should be thought of as a one page commercial advertisement about you. It should include any relevant past experience to your voice work. The resume needs to have your contact phone number and email address. Refrain from a chronological listing of your past experience, better to list the job then the date. I prefer resumes that have three interesting pieces of information per experience. It's quality over quantity when it comes to your promotional material. Like many newcomers to voice-overs, you may not have extensive experience to list. Don't worry. Your life experience is unique to you. It got you to this point. The resume is a reflection of who you are as a person, not just what you've done. Also, remember that the resume's main purpose is to motivate the reader to listen to your demo. Think about it: the package gets opened, the CD goes into the player, computer or hyperlink address or what have you, then the resume is glanced over while your demo is playing. The resume is meant to help fill in the picture of who you are. There are hundreds of resume examples found on the web. Find one that looks right for you. (You can use the format on page 98 if you like). Ask a trusted professional their impression of your resume. Be careful not to ask too many people for their opinions though...it will lead to frustration.

The final piece of your marketing package is the cover letter. It works best when it is brief and to the point. It must be addressed to a specific person, never "to whom it may concern". If you are not sure who the responsible recipient is, call and find out. The best cover letters are ones in which there is an additional reason for the correspondence other than "I need a job". For example, "I was reading an article about you and was impressed with your frank assessment about...". Or, "My sister's best friend is a mutual acquaintance and she recommended..." Remember that the cover letter is the initial handshake (or slate!) in what could be a great relationship. Put yourself in the place of the receiver. How would you respond if you received your package? A careful, objective scrutiny of your presentation materials is critical to your success. Professionalism goes a long way with those who may avail themselves of your services. That said, marketing your materials is a great first step to accomplish.

The question now becomes "who do I send or email it to?" Lets look at who's looking. The next page includes a chart that breaks down the industry into easily identifiable components. Notice "you" at the bottom of the page. The arrows point to various "players" that are the decision makers when it comes to booking voice-over talent. (Continued on page 83)

Workshop Workout

Voice-over job seeker flowchart

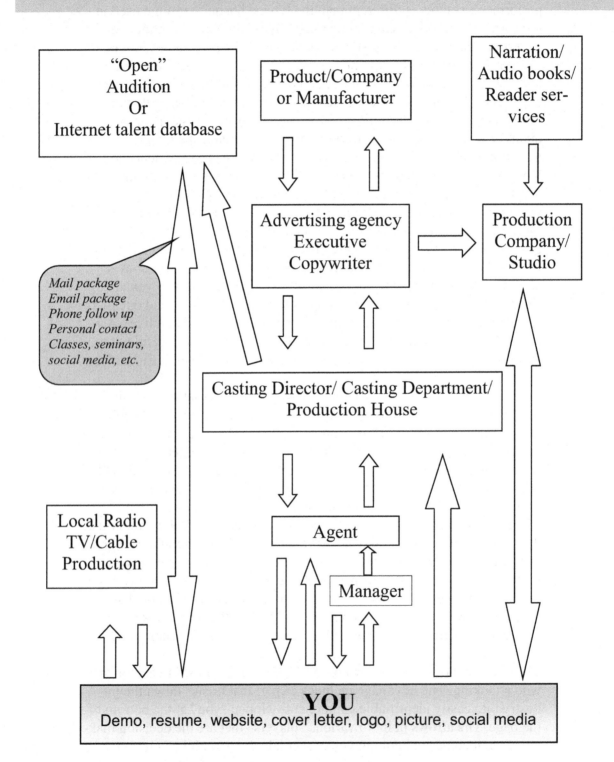

As you can see, there are several ways to get a booking. One step is to make contact with your local radio and TV/Cable stations. Many of these resources go uninvestigated by newcomers to the industry. Most stations often produce their own local commercials and sometimes appreciate voice actor help with their spots. Although there may be little or even no money involved, getting the experience and having your work "on air" is a plus. The same goes for local TV and cable outlets. Just by letting production departments at these facilities know about you can achieve positive responses. Open auditions, commercial production companies and advertising agencies are other ways you can bypass having an agent and establish yourself as a professional voice talent. I try to remember that work begets work!

Larger markets such as metropolitan areas will often have talent agents who use voice-over actors as part of their stable of available talent for booking. Depending on the geographical size of the area, there may be just a few agents who fit this category. Legitimate agents will charge ten percent of the revenue for the work they get for you. They often are signatories of the performance unions (Screen Actors Guild, SAG and/or American Federation of Television Artists, AFTRA). Strict rules with respect to payment, work environment, use of talent, pay for play, etc. are adhered to. This does not mean that you must be a member of the union. It does mean that the agent has a professional obligation to treat all of their talent respectfully. If you are not a member of the performers union, consider this: there are many opportunities for you to get hired without being a member of the union. Agents are allowed to work with non-union talent. Joining the union does not guarantee you employment or even increase the number of job opportunities that might be available. In fact, union statistics on unemployment among its membership usually hover around 98%.

So, if your interest is in getting experience and growing your list of credits, focus on what makes the most sense for you. Unions cost money to join, take a percentage of your gross earnings and preclude you from non-union jobs. Developing your contacts, getting the word out and marketing your talent might be the best, most logical first step you need to take.

Exercise:
Page 82 contains the voice-over job seekers flowchart. As you evaluate your professional options, consider the many varied paths you may choose to take. It helps to plan your strategy with a business plan as if you are the CEO of your own company. You are the product and your talent is the service!

Managers belong in a slightly different category than agents. It is important to know the difference. This unique relationship may not just include voice talent, but actors, singers, dancers and celebrities as well. Managers function exactly as the name implies; They *manage* your career. Agents represent you, the talent, while managers work *through* the agents for the benefit of the talent they represent. This distinction is often made muddy by those that would seek to exploit the unsuspecting talent. The idea of a manager for some would seem exciting, professional and perceived as an advancement to your career. This may not necessarily be the case. There are many professional managers who are truly interested in your career development. They will often have track records of successful industry relationships that can be quite impressive. The only problem is that anyone can call themselves a manager. Additionally, they can take whatever percentage of your earnings that you agree to. Agents, on the other hand, are required by union regulations to adhere to standards and professional practices. (exceptions to this are prevalent and caution must be used). Managers are compensated over and above what would go to an agent, usually 15 percent or more.

While it may seem that I am sounding a bit down on the use of managers, this is not the case. I believe that managers can be extremely valuable to the talent they represent. For example, if there is so much work that it becomes difficult to sort out the best career move, a manager can be quite an asset. If the manager has a solid track record, successful business ethics and reliable advice, then this may be a wise relationship to develop. Remember that for legitimate union jobs, managers must use a franchised agent to negotiate for the talent. You may be spending more for a manager (after all it is you who hire both the agent and manager with the money you make) so it makes sense if they are grooming your career, promoting your talent and providing opportunities that you might not otherwise have available to you.

Casting directors fit into a different category that can confuse some performers. Here is a simple rule to keep in mind to understand the difference between agents and casting directors: agents are hired by the actor to promote the actor while casting directors are hired by the producer to find the right talent for the job. Agents do their best to "pitch" their talent for the job by consulting a *breakdown,* (listings of job requests) sent by casting directors or producers. Casting directors have an obligation to provide the best choices available for what the producer is requesting. Voice-over casting directors might be hired by the advertising agency on a "per job/client" basis. Larger advertising agencies might have their own casting department. In either case, there is no harm in letting the casting director know about you through mail, email or personal contact as long as it is done in a professional way.

84

Most of the time casting directors are too busy to spend much time with you. In this time of economic uncertainty, everyone is trying very hard to please their clients. Casting directors are no different. Some may strictly use agents, in which case you would be well advised not to try and pitch your demo. Others might keep a library of unrepresented talent. Still others may search the internet. This could be a good thing for you if you are just starting out.

Another entity for you to connect with is the production company. They are the producers of commercials, audio books, promotional advertisements, video games, etc. They often have a production person in charge of finding the talent for their various projects. Sending a package to them with a follow-up email is a good way to make a positive impression. Remember that the package you send to these folks does not get you the job. It will, hopefully, get you an audition. It may get you a place in their files for a "yet to be determined" project. It may also get no attention at all. The best thing for your sanity is to understand how each of these various entities work. Sending a professional looking package, having a clean presentation on your website and a demo that is marketable will put you into the best possible circumstances for voice-over opportunities.

While there is no magic formula for success, there are common traits that can be found with any successful performer. One is perseverance. I am sure you have heard how keeping a clear, focused objective will eventually pay off. While this is often true, I would like to add one more aspect to this viewpoint; maintaining a realistic appraisal of the business. This is vital to success as well. Being determined to succeed is noble and commendable. However, having a realistic understanding of how the business works, using the right tools and the ability to maintain a professional outlook is what really works for many, many successful voice talents I have met. Taking a systematic approach to your business plan can also help alleviate the excessive stress that usually affects the newcomer or professional that is taking on another career path. It is one thing to have talent and performance sensibilities, it is quite another to develop the various business aspects into an equally sustainable and satisfying model of success.

Jeff's notebook

Sometimes ad agencies or production houses will put together a test spot. They want to see if the client likes the concept before committing to a full ad campaign. They often hire actors to voice these sample commercials or concepts. The pay is very low, $100 or less. I always say yes to these. Great experience, professional connections, and on more than one occasion I ended up with a booking.

Workshop Workout

Business checklist for success

Use this page to check off each of these criteria for establishing your Voice-over business

I Have...

☐ Read this book and understand the principles of performance and production.
☐ Completed the workbook pages.
☐ Assembled material that reflects my "cast-ability" talent and demographic.
☐ Rehearsed each choice for variety and versatility.
☐ Recorded the voice tracks of my material in a professional way.
☐ Edited and produced (by me or another) my demo into a professional CD.
☐ Made a list of professional contacts for mailing/emailing/calling.
☐ Created and assembled my cover letter, resume, demo material with a professional look.
☐ Added my demo, resume, picture, references to a website of my Voice-over business.
☐ Marketed my material to everyone on my professional contact list.

I Will...

☐ Promote, maintain, market the business professionally.
☐ Attend every audition and opportunity that is available.
☐ Follow up every audition and opportunity with a thank you email or note.
☐ Continue to update, rehearse, read out loud, material that I may be called upon to audition for.

Other essential business materials to consider:

- Business cards
- 8X10 Professional headshot: The actors standard equipment is also used in VO's because It lends credibility to your professional image.
- Resume
- Business/company logo
- Business stationery including CD envelopes and labels
- Email address/ professional website with links
- Social media page (Facebook, Linkedin, Youtube, etc.)
- CD Labels for your demo (no jewel cases...too much breakage)
- Brochure of your company (mailing)
- Press release with biography announcing your company/story
- Recording studio equipment

Clearly, some of these items may not fit into your plan. It is up to you to decide, of course. Just know that for those who intend to leap into the professional arena, having this list will assist with the typical requests you will receive from the industry at the outset.

Hold Your Ears

Now is the time for me to share some conclusions about this workshop. While I have done my best to include as much information as I can about voice-overs into a comprehensive and accessible format, there is always something more to add. It's as if every relevant experience I have gone through has to be included for fear of omitting a vital piece of information that could prove useful. So, I have decided to write this chapter for just such occasions. Bits of advice and suggestions that somehow got left out and end up as an afterthought. Perhaps you will find some little gem or nugget that will answer a lingering question. Additionally, since no two journeys are alike, there are items that you just might find useful while on your own voyage.

I used to spend countless hours wondering why the audition I just gave did not produce a booking. Clearly, I was never completely satisfied with any audition unless it produced results...namely a callback or booking. It simply wasn't enough to do well. Rather, the measure of my success was based on tangible results. I put myself under tremendous pressure to succeed. I also felt that if I didn't "win" the job then I might not be thought of by my agent the next time an opportunity came up. I was concerned that the casting director might not like me. I was certain that with every success, a rash of failure was inevitable. Wow! What a trip. It took some time but what I did eventually discover was that my thoughts didn't matter. Feelings were not facts. The measure of my success was based on a false premise that being talented was the same as being successful. This is not the case. Many talented performers do not get the big prize. Conversely, I have seen many, not so talented, performers do unbelievably well. There is no formula for success. It is a mystery, an enigma, a random selection not given to logic. The best thing to do is to fully accept this reality. Embrace the notion that what is considered successful or not is of your own making. Being prepared with the right materials, confident within yourself, approachable and pleasant is the key to fulfillment. As I write these words I can see that it is easy to present the concept but, frankly, it takes a lifetime to achieve. I still need to practice being accepting of situations out of my control. Keeping the focus on the work and *not* my interpretation of how I am doing has brought me to a place of understanding. I love so many aspects of this business and now, I can really enjoy the process. My wish is that you can make similar discoveries for yourself.

When I received word that I had won a job, booking or gig, I tried to recall the events surrounding my behavior and approach to that particular audition. I thought that if I could remember *what* I had done, then recreating the moment would lead to more bookings. This was a fool's errand; I found no parallels with my approach to each successful audition. Again, randomness won out over process. Again, I learned that being prepared, confident and pleasant were the only requirements that made sense when the opportunity presented itself.

We actors are often sensitive to rejection. After all, not getting the job is interpreted as a rejection of our talent, or worse, personal failure. Yet, we are asked to be vulnerable and "available" to any and all choices for the characters we are playing. Conversely, the demands of the profession are such that having a thick business skin is necessary for survival. Which is it? Sensitive artist or business bully? My best guess is that we evolve into a bit of both over time. If we can sustain and nurture our talent, then we can wear both hats successfully. It is not one or the other but both which are needed for our survival.

When you have an audition, meeting or introduction, make sure you reinforce the relationship with a "thank you". A hand-written card or personal email will go a long way with the relationships you are developing. Get into the habit of this and it won't seem like a hassle. This type of professional courtesy is, believe it or not, rarely done. Your confidence and credibility will grow with these acts of kindness.

Keep your voice demo fresh by adding new material to it. It can be a piece you add after a booking (provided it is of superior quality) or something you produce on your own. Like your picture and resume which is ever changing, the demo needs to be thought of in the same way.

It may seem odd, but keep a professional wardrobe separate from your everyday clothing. I know, we're talking voice-over's...heard but not seen right? Well, consider that with each audition (unless it's online) comes a face to face meeting with someone who may be in a position to recommend you. Don't miss an opportunity by looking less than your best. A discriminating decision is made about you within fifteen seconds of meeting.

Jeff's notebook

Inevitably, the audition that I want the most is the harder one to get. I think it's because there is a sense of desperation attached to my read. The spots that are easy for me end up being the ones I book. Go figure. Desperation never produces a good outcome. Now, if I could only remember that...

What drives you to be a performer? Is it fame? Is it money? Is it about having fun? I suppose any combination of these concepts are valid. For me, I am passionate about my work. I love every opportunity that gives me a chance to *show my stuff.* "Passion is what drives me most." This phrase is a liner that I wrote in one of our scripted sections in this book. It really does answer the question for me. Being passionate about something is a feeling like no other. As a professional, you must assume that talent is a given. Everyone is talented. The difference between your talent and another actor's talent is your technique and uniqueness. You can hone and refine your technique by studying, interpreting your own personal experiences and performing. Your uniqueness is another matter. You might think that you are who you are. That you cannot *learn* how to be different. That you cannot change who you are as an actor or person. In my view, this is not the case. We are capable of shifting how the world perceives us. By virtue of embracing what it is to be an actor, we can become malleable, transformative, special. That is what I find most amazing. Only by understanding that we are flexible will we begin to define ourselves as unique individual entities. It is passion that defines the degree to which I choose to enhance how the world perceives me and my talent.

I am grateful for many things. Near the top of my list is having a sense of humor. It has saved me countless times in the past. Finding the humor in otherwise mundane, ordinary and boring situations is key to my survival. My wish for you is to really look at your own ability to laugh. Laugh at yourself. Laugh at others. Laugh at situations. Knowing what is funny and what can become funny becomes quite a gift. This is especially true in this rather strange world of voice acting. It's amazing; one day you are selling toilet tissue, the next day you are telling folks about the virtues of sobriety in a public service announcement. Keep a proper perspective and let your humor be a supporting partner in your work and in your life.

Now it's time for us to rewrite the introduction to this book...

Hamlet:
Come give us a taste of your quality, come, a passionate
speech.

Re-visiting the

Intro

It feels more like the waiting room of a dentist's office than a voice-over audition. Half a dozen actors nervously mouth the words into their crumpled script. YOU walk in, smiling. You look great in your new shirt and casual/professional appearance. Because you are early to your session, you have time to casually greet the other actors. After all, you have seen each one at different times and at various auditions. They are more like friendly acquaintances. The casting director comes out of the studio into the waiting room and breathes a sigh of relief. She is genuinely happy to see you. You quietly take a seat and review the material with confidence. When it is your turn to walk into the recording studio, you feel welcomed by the suits behind the glass. After all, they hope you will be the one voice they are looking for. When your audition is done you feel really good that you have been able to provide your point of view with your best interpretation. You politely thank each person, including the engineer, and exit quickly with purpose. On your exit you make sure you write down your performance notes, who was at the audition, and remember to call your agent with the good news about your successful session. Welcome to the world of the successful voice-over artist.

Jeff's Notebook

The creative performer benefits most when they view themselves not only as an artisan, but as a business person, using their ability to effectively transform their talent into tangible, meaningful tools and skills embraced by the marketplace.

Workshop Cleanup

Jeffrey directing a VO session at CDM Studios, New York, NY

On the following pages are some additional ***workshop workouts*** that you may find useful. I have also repeated some pages that you have already seen. Each page is meant to address specific areas that are important to re-visit or use more than once. You may elect to photocopy them (for just yourself of course) and keep them handy, or leave them in the book. You may elect to cut out the ones in the back and use them without pulling the book apart and thereby destroying useful information. Whichever you choose, I hope it helps.

The next page is my personal version of VO record keeping. I like to have as much information in one central location as I can. I refer to these quite often when I need to know what choices I made at an audition or who to send a thank you note to. Over time, the same contacts seem to repeat themselves. I realize how small this business is and how the players connect together. It is also a good way to remind myself that this is a business that depends on me being organized.

On another note, try to keep your audition copy if you can. It becomes a wonderful tool for keeping yourself sharp and confident. It doesn't matter whether you got the job or not. It will serve as a catalog of your journey. After all, isn't it fair that for every audition there should be a reward? I'm just sayin'...

Activity Log

Contacts   **Classes**   **Meetings**

Auditions   **Sessions**   **Rehearsals**

Date	Who: Name/Phone:	1st Meet	What: Purpose:	Where: Location/Address:	Notes: Remember:
	I feel creative within the copy				
	Work at staying present Whisper the copy. when practising - overeducate				

Spontaneity

NOTES:

Workshop Workout

Voice-over Media checklist

Complete each checkbox as they happen. Provide as much detail as you can about the performance style and persona of the voice you experience. Add as many different media and subjects as you experience them in the spaces below.

☑	DATE	TIME	MEDIA	SUBJECT/STYLE/PERSONA
			Phone Recording	
			Website	
			Radio	
			Television Commercial	
			Live	
			Toys/games	
			Audio books	
			Narration (recorded)	
			Film Looping	
			TV or Cable Promo (station promotional announcement or station promotion)	
			Film Trailer	

Workshop Workout

Radio/TVspotStoryboard with Script

☐ TV ☐ Radio ☐ Other media _____

Time: :30

*Name of product:*_____*Author:*_____

Production notes: _____

Music/Storyboard graphic/SFX	:00 VO:

Music/Storyboard graphic/SFX	:05

Music/Storyboard graphic/SFX	:10

Music/Storyboard graphic/SFX	:15

Music/Storyboard graphic/SFX	:20

Music/Storyboard graphic/SFX	:25

Music/Storyboard graphic/SFX	:30

Workshop Workout

Home Run or Fowl out
Useful tips to keep in mind when you audition or get hired.

DO	DON'T
Arrive early, square breathe, apply cold reading techniques and enjoy the process.	Arrive late, dress sloppily, talk to friends, "wing it".
Enter the room positively, place your copy on the stand, put on cans, don't speak.	Saunter in, try to be, "chatty", blow into the mic, ask questions before starting.
If requested, give a level by performing the *last* few sentences of a script full out.	Say, "Test, Test, 1,2,3,4...I am talking now...into the microphone..."
Slate your name with energy as yourself. (Smile)	Slate in a character or funny voice, depressed, uninterested, casual.
Take a beat (pause) before and after your slate.	Rush into the copy after the slate.
Know the name of the product, who is talking and the mood of the copy.	Mess up the name of the product, sound like you are reading, lack truthful energy.
Take a clear point of view.	Be general and hope they can get the general idea.
Perform your copy while speaking to one specific person.	Announce your copy.
End the copy on an up note (positive, hopeful, optimistic).	Drop your energy before you are finished.
Say, "Would you like it more (pick one) warm, upbeat, character?"	Ask for a re-take, ask, "How's that?... Do you want me to do it again?"

Workshop Workout

Notation:	Used for:	Means:
_____ (Underline)	Pronunciation/Take note	This needs special attention
↗ (arrow up)	Inflection	Raise the voice pitch
↘ (arrow down)	Inflection	Lower the voice pitch
// (hash marks)	Timing	Gear change
/ (single slash)	Timing	Pause (breath)
◯ (circle)	Pronunciation	Potential pitfall
! (exclamation mark)	Punctuation	Stress the point

BELOW: You can devise you own method of marking. Just make sure you remember what they stand for!

Other marks to consider:

Pitch ∧∧ Variety, voice ↻ slide, Product name, ☆ Warm/sexy/smile. ♡

Notation:	Used for:	Means:

Workshop Workout

Commercial Voice-over demo Sample checklist

List the best choices you have for placement in your commercial demo. Next, arrange the choices in numerical order with check boxes selected for definitions/options to consider. Remember that production variety and vocal versatility are the important factors to consider, while contrasting choices are equally important factors to consider. Your choices should reflect your abilities and casting potential. This is meant to be an example and may not work for every category of commercial demo!

⏱ Name of Spot:	#	Character/ Personality	Production Elements:

Bookable/Bankable ☐

Fun/Light ☐

Character ☐

Straight Announce ☐

Driving/Fast ☐

Sincere/ Empathetic ☐

Fun/Light ☐

Unusual/ Off beat ☐

Animation ☐

Notes: _____

_____

_____

_____

⏱ _____

TOTAL TIME :<:60   Slate/Out take:_____

# Workshop Workout

Voice-over Resume Layout Sample

Here is a sample resume form for you to consider. Use your own creative flair to add or remove items as you see fit. Remember that this is a one page advertisement about you. It must be easy to read and formatted for clarity and relational to your goals.

Optional Picture

Your Name
Actor & Voice talent

Contact phone: Social media address:
Email address: Website: www.yourname.com

Professional Background and Experience

Job type or name	Character Played	Producer/location
Job type or name	Character Played	Producer/location
Job type or name	Character Played	Producer/location

Education and Training

School/Class	Location	Course covered
School/Class	Location	Course covered
Voice-over workshop	Jeffrey Dreisbach	VO intensive

Employment

Employment	Location	Date
Employment	Location	Date
Employment	Location	Date

Special Skills and Interests

- Useful skill
- Useful skill
- Useful skill

Biographical Statement

Highly motivated, creative performer with exemplary work ethic and professional training.

Voice-over Demo Compilation enclosed

98

Acknowledgements

Writing a book is truly a collaborative effort. So many students, teachers and friends have been invaluable with their comments, suggestions and meaningful contributions that it would be impossible to list them all. Suffice it to say that I am truly grateful to everyone who helped propel this project "dream" into reality. Below are listed some special people whose assistance and guidance have helped shape and define this publication. Thank you!

CDM Studios, NY
Josh Andrews
Suellen Vance
Rick Wasserman
Anna Sofar
Andrew Duff
Sally Dunn
Terry Schreiber
Pat McCorkle
Theodore Sweats
Sandy Robbins
Dale A.J. Rose
Enrique Gonzalez
Penny Molyneux

UMKC 2011 MFA actors:
Zachary Andrews
Noel Collins
Cat Endsley
Dina Kirsch
Eric Gravez
Amy Urbina
Mark Thomas

Please feel free to contact me with your questions or comments. Although I have done by best in providing you with useful, practical information, I am sure their will always be room for additional insight and feedback. I would be especially grateful for any success stories you might have experienced as a result of your VO efforts. You can contact me via my website, ***www.jeffreydreisbach.com*** or via email at ***jeffreydreisbach@gmail.com***

Thanks and good luck!

CPSIA information can be obtained
at www.ICGtesting.com
Printed in the USA
LVOW03s2045120516
487994LV00011B/22/P